The art of living
to the fullest

Dear reader:

After you finish reading this book, we would love to
hear your opinion about it, your feedback is important
to us. Write to contato@editoraor.com

Have a good reading!

Jane Krüger, PhD

The art of living to the fullest

The path to reach an Undisturbed Soul

1st Edition

EDITORA 'OR

Publisher: Editora 'Or
Cover: Devon Tecnologia
Design: Luiz Inácio
Revision: Jane Krüger and Luiz Inácio
Photography: Yuri Nunes
Printing: Amazon Kindle Direct Publishing
Translation: Vinicius Freire and Igor Romani Fracalossi

Dados Internacionais de Catalogação na Publicação (CIP)
(Câmara Brasileira do Livro, SP, Brasil)

```
Krüger, Jane
   The art of living to the fullest : the path to
reach an undisturbed soul / Jane Krüger ;
[translation Vinicius Freire, Igor Romani
Fracalossi]. -- 1. ed. -- Bento Gonçalves, RS :
Editora 'Or, 2022.

   Título original: A arte de viver plenamente : o
caminho para alcançar uma alma imperturbável.
   Bibliografia.
   ISBN 978-65-990623-4-6

   1. Autoconhecimento 2. Desenvolvimento pessoal
3. Espiritualidade 4. Método socrático 5. Saúde
mental 6. Sucesso I. Título.

22-116815                                  CDD-158.1
```

Índices para catálogo sistemático:

1. Desenvolvimento pessoal : Psicologia   158.1

Eliete Marques da Silva - Bibliotecária - CRB-8/9380

Phone number: +55 (54) 9 9660-9422
E-mail: contato@editoraor.com
Website: www.editoraor.com

*This work is dedicated to the life and memory of **Gertrudes Krüger Hepperle.***

Inspired by her, I started writing this book, which began by the twentieth first chapter: **What memories will you leave?**

"Everything that reminds me of you relates to a strong dedication in joyfully serving others with resolute faith and deep unconditional love."

Sumário

Chapter 1

Chapter 2

Chapter 3

Chapter 4

Chapter 5

Chapter 9

Chapter 10

Chapter 11

Chapter 12

Chapter 13

Chapter 14

Chapter 15

Chapter 16

Chapter 17

Chapter 18

Chapter 19

Chapter 20

Chapter 21

PREFACE

Reflecting to live and to be better

Defining Philosophy is not an easy task. The very question "What is philosophy?" is, by itself, a philosophical question. One of many possible answers is considering Philosophy as a special kind of attitude towards existence, the action of thinking about moral life, a devotion to contemplate the world in order to learn from it, and by doing so, living your life in a wiser, more ethical way. Philosophy would then be less of a theoretical exercise and more of a practical way of pursuing a sensible life, a lesson on how we could conquer ourselves, our impulses. By peering into human vices and passions, into freedom and will, thus offering our rationale the knowledge needed to impose boundaries to our cravings and desires, Philosophy would aim to teach us about virtue, which is the principle of the good life. It is precisely in this sense that Socrates stated that the unexamined life is not worth living.

In *The Art of Living to the Fullest*, Dra. Jane Krüger retakes this traditional philosophical conception to offer her readers a series of tools for self-analysis and self-discovery. Using the Socratic method, she provokes us with the right questions about apparently trivial topics. How are the people you interact with daily? How do you react to hard times? What is preventing you from accomplishing what you want? Are you happy with yourself? Do you do to others what you wish others would do to you? What about your meals? Are you using your time well? Under the surface of these innocent questions, there is a foggy maze, indistinguishable from the dark corners of our minds, and through this reading, the author will cleverly show us the way, with the aid of many psychological theories, schools of thought, and spiritual doctrines, and supporting the established conclusions with a careful selection of sayings from mankind's most enlightened minds. Consequently, with such a multifaceted approach, the misleading paths and dead ends of our inner paths will be dissolved, better yet, reshaped into new ways, this time with less walls and more bridges to connect areas of our psyche that were once secluded.

What is beyond doubt, however, is that a book like *The Art of Living to the Fullest* cannot be described as an instruction manual for your life or even a script for personal success, especially because you will not find here guides, tips, or answers. What you will find here are lots of questions, so, if we must use any metaphor to define Dra. Jane Krüger's work, we should think of it as a map or a compass, which are only there to guide those who already know where they are going. For them, this reading will also be a reflective practice, and combined with real actions, it will certainly lead to a genuine path.

History tells us that, in the 15th century, Ermolao Barbaro, an Italian scholar, summoned the Devil in order to obtain from him an explanation for what Aristotle really meant to achieve with his term entelechy, which is related to the purpose of any person in this universe, to the true final accomplishment in a natural sense, a guide and a definitive point of the changing process every person goes through. At least to what concerns human beings, *The Art of Living to the Fullest* releases us from the need of using any Mephistophelian tricks to gain knowledge about what could be, in essence, this supposed perfect state: it is merely about becoming what we truly want to be, deep inside. What remains now is how we can achieve it. What route should we take to get there? This is the challenge that awaits us in the next pages.

Rafael Bán Jacobsen
President of Academia
Rio-Grandense de Letras

January 2020

I had the honour and privilege of meeting Dr. Jane Krüger in Israel where I was introduced to her new book. She's a gifted writer, talented speaker and a leading psychoanalyst in her field. Her personal story will bring you to tears as it did with me. Her life's achievements will inspire you to reach your higher potential. Anyone with a painful past will be able to identify with her book and be mesmerised by the resilience of her story on every page. This book has changed the way I look at trauma and has changed the way I understand the world around me, for the better. You will be speaking about this book for months after you finish reading it.

Massimo Gabriele Zohar Bialyk
Spiritual leader of the New Hasidic Jewish
Community in Israel an Jewish genealogist.

INTRODUCTION

We are living days of amazing technological breakthrough. Things were never so quickly developed, we buy a piece of high-tech equipment in one day, and the next day, something far more advanced is being offered to us.

Even with all this information and knowledge now available at the touch of a button, humans have never felt so lonely, anguished, depressed and anxious. Furthermore what is most alarming, new mental disorders are coming every day like a plague.

We are overwhelmed with resources, and yet, we feel empty, lost, deprived of emotions and satisfying experiences.

Even though we have so much, as unbelievable as it sounds, our lives still seem meaningless. We feel poor, we wander like beggars inside our hearts.

As terrifying as it may seem, we have reached a point where we are able to build machines that surpass our own intelligence, but we stripped ourselves of the greatest ingenuity, the Art of Living.

We are surrounded by high-tech devices and we have access to thousands of bits of information at every second. Not only are we connected twenty-four hours a day, but we have become, in a way, extremely dependent on these new tools, and little by little, without even noticing, we are losing what is most valuable to us. We are disconnecting from ourselves. We have forgotten our essence.

We have lost sight of things. We have damaged our capacity to see what is important in life: the simplest things. We look at complex things and seek meaning, we look at innovations and seek inspiration.

We hear so many things, so many voices, that we have become insensitive, deaf to human voices. Among our excessive consumerism, we are horrified, hypnotized, and stunned. We do not know where to go, what to look, what to seek. There are so many paths, so many options, we are soaked and fatigued.

In the end, nothing is ever good enough, nothing will sate us, nothing is satisfying anymore, and we easily lose our will to live. There is an alarming rate of suicides lately, especially among teenagers. The rate of suicides has been increasing and all seems normal in this crazy life we are living.

We lost the ability to reflect, to feel, to love, to compromise, to give ourselves. We have unlearned how to handle things. Yes, we have unlearned, we have lost the ability to live.

This book is not a magic potion that will allow you to happily hop and sing around, laughing as you wake up in a colorful world where you will have everything you need and where you will find all the answers to the uncertainties of your life. If that is what you are looking for, I am terribly sorry to tell you, this book is going to disappoint you a lot.

This book will ask you many questions. You will probably not like them. Perhaps nobody will. And these questions will be hard to answer. They will make you think. Maybe a lot. So much so that it will provoke some changes. Instead of making you laugh, they will probably make you cry. But this is not all bad. Tears can clean and heal us. Tears can erase a page of your life that is all blurry or scrawled. They can give you a new sheet of paper for a new beginning.

This book has a single purpose: to make you more conscious. To turn you into a human again.

Yes. Human, in your essence.

We were turned into machines.

Machines that eat, buy and work.

Machines, not humans.

This book will make you reflect on quite simple yet extremely meaningful things, what is essential if you want to live your life to the fullest. It will bring back to you the sensitivity of a real human.

In our global, interconnected and technological community, we have lost our humanity (unbelievable, right?). We have lost our sensitivity to see how beautiful life is.

I encourage you, dear reader, to go through these next pages and let these simple words carry you on, allowing you to fall in love with the magnificence and beauty of the greatest gift we have received: our Lives.

My deepest and most sincere prayer is that the Eternal, The Creator of the Universe may bring into your heart his own pulsating life, along with joy, passion, abundant love, so that you may truly be the greatest act of his creation: A HUMAN.

I wrote this book to you with deep love and tenderness.

Jane Krüger

Shalom!

Chapter 1

THINKING THE RIGHT WAY

"If the head is useless, the rest you may throw away."

Yiddish Saying

1

Thinking the right way is, without a doubt, one of the secrets to live life. To truly live, that is. Because unfortunately, most people are not living their lives, they are just existing.

Life is a daily labor, hourly even. And the fundamentals for everything we build in life are based on our own thoughts. Wrong, false, or inadequate thoughts lead us to poor decisions, misleading paths, bad relationships, which in turn lead to frustrations and deeper disappointments, and if these issues are not effectively managed and solved, they can become a dead end, a tunnel with no end in sight.

"...most people are not living their lives; they are just existing."

Accumulated Frustrations = Distorted Point of View

Multiple disappointments will easily turn into a systematic construction of a distorted view of ourselves and consequently, of others. Slowly, we start to shut ourselves. We become smaller. Isolated. Thoughts will break into our minds, causing an exhaustive turmoil, echoing the same words day and night: "I was not blessed in this life, there is no point in fighting anymore, I was not born to shine, I have to contend with what I have, everything I do leads nowhere....", and this way, those vague ponderations may turn into beliefs that will boycott our personal stories. We give up without even trying to develop our potential.

Your potential is like a ball of wool in a handicraft shop. It has potential to become a nice sweater or scarf, however, many times it does not even leave the shelf.

We must think the right way.

The source of boycotting thoughts

Thoughts are not randomly created, they are there because they were planted in our minds by our experiences, traumas, what we have heard from others and what we tell ourselves. However, after they have been planted, they must also be fed. If we do not feed them, they will weaken and die, thus ceasing to influence over our lives. So, for a thought to be strong, it needs sustenance. If, during your whole life, you have heard negative words like "You are nobody, you will achieve nothing, everything you do is wrong, you are one big mess to this world", let me just tell you this: make a decision to not feed those words anymore, detach yourself from them, stop repeating them and perpetuating them in your mind. To do this, let me give you this recipe below:

Replace the Food!

You can choose who you want to be, but you must genuinely believe that. You need to change your thoughts. To replace your food. If you start believing you are someone truly loved, who is not here in this world for nothing, but instead was designed by the Creator of Life with a specific purpose, a special and unique role to play here on Earth, if you believe and truly feel these things, you could be someone who makes all the difference in the world. You will make a difference for someone, or even for millions of people.

Your choice!

All Depends on Your Belief

Life is worth living; however, it will only truly be worth it if you honestly believe it! Every minute is unique, it will not come back. Life is our biggest treasure, and it is a divine gift. Choose to believe in this and be thankful for existing, for being alive in this exact moment in time. There is a purpose in this fact too. So, do not waste your days with petty and inadequate thoughts that will not lift you up, will not make you grow, and will not be fruitful to your life.

I encourage you to:

Choose to be your best version today!

Stop existing and start living.

LIVING!

Personal analysis

"What negative thoughts have been living in my mind that could be boycotting my happiness, my plans, and my dreams?" Reflect on it and write down below. Put on paper the thoughts you think have been afflicting, sabotaging, diminishing you.

____

____

____

____

____

____

____

____

____

____

____

____

____

____

____

____

Task

1. Choose to be the best version of yourself from this moment on. Write down below which areas of your life and which thoughts you have decided to change to do your best, and say out loud:

I SWEAR TO BE THE BEST VERSION OF MYSELF FROM NOW ON, STARTING BY:

____

____

____

____

____

____

____

____

____

____

____

____

____

____

____

____

____

2. Read the answers to the question above for the next 21 days. This will help you remember your new goal to become your best version. You can also transcribe them into a sheet of paper or a poster and even illustrate it. Then, place it somewhere you get to see every day, always repeating the words out loud.

3. Determine that:

I am what I wish to be.

I will not be my best version soon,

I will be my best version NOW.

Thoughts for meditation

"We think too much and feel too little.
More than machinery, we need humanity.
More than cleverness, we need kindness and gentleness.
Without these qualities, life will be violent, and all will be lost."

Charles Chaplin

English Actor, Dancer, Director, and Producer.
He was the most famous artist of the silent era of movie.

"Thinking is the hardest work there is.
Which is probably the reason so few engage in it."

Henry Ford

Prolific inventor, he registered 161 patents
in the United States. Founder of Ford.

"He who thinks little errs much..."

Leonardo da Vinci

Extraordinary Italian polymath.
He was a scientist, mathematician, engineer,
inventor, anatomist, painter, sculptor, architect,
botanist, poet, and musician.

.

*"The less men think,
the more they talk."*

Charles de Montesquieu

French politician, philosopher, and writer.

*"We are what we think.
All we are arises with our thoughts.
With our thoughts, we make the world."*

Siddhartha Gautama

Buddha, spiritual master,
founder of Buddhism.

"I have thoughts which, if I could bring them forth and make them living, would add a new lightness to the stars, a new beauty to the world, and a greater love to the heart of men."

Fernando Pessoa

Modern Portuguese Poet,
Politician, and literary critic.

Chapter 2

THE RIGHT PEOPLE

"

*"Bad companies are like a fish market. Eventually,
we will get used to the smell."*

Yiddish Saying

2

The right people are the ones who love you, appreciate you, and accept you for who you are, not for what you have. They encourage you to go beyond, to evolve in your life and in areas that you consider important. The right people are the ones who, once you leave their presence, you feel more alive than ever, they are a walking stimulant, they are the energy dose that recharges you and they will give you the push you need to proceed.

> *"The right people are the ones who, once you leave their presence, you feel more alive than ever..."*

The right people will love you and accept you even when you make mistakes - they understand life is a learning process, where the crucial thing is to get up after falling, while learning not to fall again.

Neuroscience proves an old saying

"Tell me with whom you consort, and I will tell you who you are". This sentence, which is a consecrated popular saying, is traditionally credited to Socrates, the great Greek philosopher. It occurred to me when I came to know the research of one of today's neuroscientists, Dr. Moran Cerf. He says when people spend too much time together, their brain waves start to look alike, and in some cases, may even become identical. He also says sharing ideas and experiences will create a feedback between these brains, and this way, two people who watch the same movies, read the same books, share the same experiences, and in addition to all this, also constantly talk to each other, by the end of two weeks, will start showing common patterns in language, emotions, and even points of view.[1]

Considering this, the best decision we can make in our lives is to carefully choose people we relate to, because one way or another, we will be like them. In a certain way, this theory endorses what Pablo Picasso used to say, that "a good painting among bad paintings will eventually become a bad painting. And a bad painting among good paintings will eventually become a good painting".

Choose wisely

We need to carefully choose the people that we engage and spend our time with. It is a clever attitude choosing to be around positive, joyful people who are in constant growth in their own lives. According to Caio Fernando Abreu, a Brazilian writer, when people close to you choose to go on their own separate way, don't be sad, this is likely an answer to the prayer: "deliver us from evil".

Not everyone is the right person to have a relationship, that is, if we want to develop ourselves, if we want to grow and to be fruitful, so we can make a difference in the world we live in. Hence,

---

1. According to neuroscientists, this is the most important decision you'll ever make. Available at https://www.countryliving.com/uk/wellbeing/news/a2213/most-important-decision-who-you-spend-time-with/ Access August 2020.

the aforementioned writer's advice is valid, and instead of regretting, step away from people who do you no good, who do not motivate you and do not stimulate your personal growth..

On the Shoulders of Giants

It is interesting to include in our list of people, those who are more mature than us, individuals who are at a higher level of knowledge and experience. We can easily settle for less if we are already the best in our environment. In a certain way, this happens because we may start to feel as if we have reached the top. So, you should try to get closer to people who are above the level

"We can easily settle for less if we are already the best in our environment."

you have already reached. This will prevent you from letting pride consume your heart, and it will instigate you to go even further. Thereby, we conclude this chapter with the great Isaac Newton, who humbly said "if I have seen further, it is by standing on the shoulders of Giants".[1]

---

1. Eco, Umberto, and Alastair McEwen. On the shoulders of giants. Cambridge, Massachusetts: The Belknap Press of Harvard University Press, 2019.

Personal analysis

1. Take a closer look at the people you most engage with. In what ways these people behave, interact, and what are their worldviews?

2. Are you proud or ashamed of these aspects?

3. Try to ponder if your current relationships will help you to become the person that you wish to become. Think about it and write your conclusions.

Task

1. Identify the people and the situations stemming from relationships that have been detrimental to you, especially if you want to become someone bigger and better.

____

____

____

____

____

____

____

2. Spend some time with the right people - this must be one of your top priorities. Write below the names of the people you consider right for your life, and in which ways you could spend more time with them.

____

____

____

____

____

____

____

Thoughts for meditation

Tehilim Psalms 1[1]

Happy is the man who has not followed the counsel of the wicked,
or taken the path of sinners, or joined the company of the insolent;
Rather, the teaching of the LORD is his delight,
and he studies that teaching day and night.

He is like a tree planted beside streams of water,
which yields its fruit in season, whose foliage never fades, and
whatever it produces thrives.

Not so the wicked; rather, they are like chaff that wind blows away.
Therefore, the wicked will not survive judgment, nor will sinners,
in the assembly of the righteous.

For the LORD cherishes the way of the righteous,
but the way of the wicked is doomed.

---

1. Sefaria.org. Psalms 1. Available at: <https://www.sefaria.org/Psalms.1?lang=bi> Accessed March 2021.

Chapter 3

HE WHO SINGS SCARES AWAY HIS WOES

"Be like the bird who, pausing in her flight awhile on boughs too slight, feels themgive way beneath her, and yet sings, knowing she hath wings."

Victor Hugo

French Novelist, poet,
playwright, and statesman.

3

I was born and raised in Brazil, in the State of Paraná, in a picturesque little town, Ipiranga. We lived in a place called, believe it or not, 'Wild Pigs'. When I was a little girl, we would not see many pigs around anymore, but in the old days, they were raised free range, were of dark color, had a black, thick fur, and their faces were similar to wild boars. Locals maintained in their houses a dry skull containing a jaw decorated with sharp teeth, probably belonging to one of these wild pigs from before.

I was never quite sure if they had this habit of hanging pig head skulls on their fences and gates out of superstition and protection or if it was just a simple reminder of a good barbecue the family had with their neighbors. Yes, because the carneação[1] was always a feast. All the neighbors were there.

After being killed, the animal had its fur shaved (with regular kitchen knives, and in a given occasion, when I was older, I even saw a lady using a razor to shave it. I must confess that scene was quite fun), the guts removed, and they washed the animal's insides with lots of water. By then, the feast was an open invitation to all, with chickens, ducks, and all sorts of birds wildly fighting for crumbles occasionally tossed to the ground, which by now would be a mix of dirt, water, blood, and discarded fur, but in a matter of seconds all of it was gone nevertheless.

---

1. Butchering

The smell was not pleasant, I never liked this part of Carneação. After the cleaning procedure, it was time to do the cutting, the meat was now tender and relaxed, hanging and waiting for the crude yet meticulously calculated cuts. Whoever was assigned to do this had an amazing knowledge of that sweet spot the knife had to hit. My parents and my two brothers are experts. I never volunteered for such a task, I bet my sisters would also not know how to do it. I remember how incredible and at the same time how dramatic was to see the animal alive before and the next minute quickly converted into valuable chunks of meat to be fondly shared with the family and the neighbors.

The best part about this festive day was at the end: there was always a barbecue and homemade bread with molasses, and for those who fancied, light cream, which I was never too fond of. Hot tea was the beverage. My mother used to say this was to keep the fat away from the stomach, so to avoid digestive problems. It usually worked that way.

It was a great celebration, but I am sure what was so jolly about it was not the meat and the barbecue, but the fact that we were all happily together. Uncles, cousins, Opa and Oma[1] were invited. Grandsons running around the yard, trying to enjoy their playtime as much as possible, and among that mild chaos, little accidents always happened to the children, it was a sure thing. At the very end, we had a lot of dishes, countless tableware, pans and basins to wash.

As the older daughter and granddaughter, usually it was my duty to do the scrubbing (one of my sisters was supposed to do the

---

1. Grandpa and Grandma in German.

washing and the third other one would do the drying, but truth be told, usually the ladies would run away from their duties, talk about a proper time to play hide-and-seek). I remember as if it were today, when all of that was finished, all those basins, the meat grinder, and all its tiny pieces parts with meat incrusted in every corner (that part wasn't nice), it was funny to look at my hands and see my whitish, wrinkled fingers, a result of warm water and soap.

The best of all was hearing the adults happily talking about daily life, about the crops, about the weather (it either rained a lot or the drought was a problem) amidst a lot of maté[1] and the smell of meat[2] being prepared. Days like those are not easily erased from our memories.

We lived in an old, small, humble wooden house. My dad was a farmer and we did not have any luxury. There was no proper shower, we showered with an aluminum bucket with a showerhead on it. I remember my mom leaving the house every day in the morning to milk the cow - many times, I enjoyed going with her and seeing her work. I clearly remember the daily rituals to tend the animals and take care of all the chores. Despite living in that modest and humble world, I remember how happy and perfect our life was. Peace prevailed there every day.

How could poor people be so happy and live so well?

---

1. A traditional brazilian beverage. Which is also known as chimarrão in Brazil, is a caffeine rich tea with antioxidants. Chimarrão is the hot infusion of Ilex paraguariensis (Portuguese: erva-mate), a South American herb, in a gourd (Portuguese: cuia). To drink it, we use a specific stainless steel straw called bomba that also works like a sieve.

2. Beef was my favorite. My grandfather had a big cattle farm.

How could poor people be so happy and live so well with so little? Even with so few possessions, it seemed as if we were short of nothing. We did not ask for a more wealthy house; I had more fun riding the cart around than I had riding the yellow VW beetle Dad bought later. How many trips we made in it! Seven people, my parents and four children (Wyllian was not born back then), and still there was always room for one more. However, the biggest question remains, what made our days so jolly?

I have the clear memory of my father, coming from the fields, with his dirty and ratty clothes, passing through the gate, always singing one of his favorite songs:

"The earth will provide if we sow it, if we do not sow, the earth will not provide, it will not provide...". And when he was not singing, he was whistling.

That joy filled the house and warmed our hearts. I do not remember a single moment in my childhood where my parents were grumbling. They went through thick and thin. There were so many lost crops, so many frustrations, and yet in their faces there was always a smile, their eyes always carried a vision that paradise could be right here on Earth, even in face of many hardships life has given them.

There were so many lost crops, so many frustrations, and yet in his face there was always a smile, his eyes always carried a vision that the paradise could be right here on Earth.

In view of all that, my conclusion is that, truthfully, we will end our day the same way we start it. If I wake up in a bad mood, fighting and cursing my own life, my job, my relationships, or any other thing, a dark cloud will appear and take possession of all the words I say. So, I should not be surprised if things easily go bad, it will obviously be a train wreck. However, if I consciously choose to be grateful, if I decide to sing instead of grumble, the dark clouds will go away and the blessings will be upon me, bringing joy and lightness to my day.

How to develop Contentment

Months are made of days. Years are made of months. If I live many consecutive days of lightness, joy, gratitude, and harmony, I have found one of the secrets of the Art of Living. This is living fully. Learning how to develop contentment and being happy despite all circumstances is the second nature to people with high levels of emotional and spiritual intelligence.

Learning how to develop contentment and being happy despite all circumstances is second nature to people with high levels of emotional and spiritual intelligence.

Many people are not living, they are just existing. They are going through life like a small boat, and depending on the current tide, they will live high and low moments, they will live peaks of excitement, and in the next minute they will see themselves about to sink, all this dictated by the environment, dictated by the circumstances.

It is About the Structure

If you decide to grow emotionally, to become more mature and sensible, by developing confidence, by choosing gratitude and contentment over grumbling and ungratefulness, by turning your attention to the good things, then everything will be different. Because all situations will have a bright side if you decide to do so, and you will not be like a small boat wandering around the big ocean of life, but rather a cruise ship that will not get affected by even the biggest storms. However, what is the main difference between that boat and the cruise ship?

The structure. A big ship has structure to handle any adversity. Our minds could be like a boat or a big ship, it all depends on the structure. The way you see life, how you see the situations and the people around you, will tell you who you are and how you live.

Quit complaining. Be thankful

If you choose singing over grumbling, you will soon notice this: LIFE WILL SPROUT BEFORE YOU. Songs about life, praise, and gratitude open the gates to Heaven on Earth. Indeed, you can have a piece of heaven in your heart. If you choose to do this, you will develop a strong, steadfast mind. This really is more valuable than diamonds. Now, if you already do

The way you see life, how do you see the situations and the people around you will tell you who you are and how you live.

that, consider yourself a millionaire. So many rich men live their lives miserably, they are so poor in spirit that even all their money cannot counterweight the impoverishment of their souls.

What is the biggest treasure we can obtain?

True wealth is not the assets or the goods we have nor the money we accumulate during life, but living our lives to the fullest, no matter what we have or how much we have, because the biggest fortune lies in being and not in having.

Learning how to sing and how to be thankful, chasing away all the woes around you is one of the secrets of the amazing art of living well. And, if he who sings scares away his woes, he who grumbles pleases his spiritual foes. Perhaps you feel shocked by my words, however countless religions and beliefs have consistently claimed we might attract good or evil to our lives depending on the words we state.

Whether you believe this or not, forces are released according to the content and weight of our words and thoughts. Recent research in Quantum Physics has proven that. Grumbling as well as cursed words will most certainly open the gates of terrible misfortunes upon our life and will give the worst spirits around the power to destroy it.

You will only reap what you sow!

Words are like seeds. As such, you may reap even one hundred for each word you sow. Let me explain. When you are a farmer and you want to grow corn, for instance, you place one or two grains of corn in the soil. Out of these seeds, a corn stalk will sprout and each stalk may produce three spikes, each one of those may contain roughly five hundred grains. Do you understand now how seeding works? You may plant one seed, but the harvest will not be in the same proportion of the sowing, it will be many times greater. Therefore, be careful with the words you place into the soil! Choose well the seed. Do not expect to get apples by planting pineapples.

Choose well the seed. Also, do not expect to get apples by planting pineapples!!

Some parents, when talking about their own children, may say:

"My son is so naughty; I don't know how to deal with him anymore...he is unbearable!"

I wonder how poor in judgment our minds can become sometimes, preventing us from reflecting on how heavy our words may be and the consequences they could bring. The Wise Solomon had already warned us, our words have the power of life and death; the one who love them will eat their fruits.[1]

---

1. Proverbs 18:21. Available at: <https://www.biblegateway.com/passage/?search=Proverbs%2018:21&version=NIV>.

A Deadly Weapon

Take this into consideration: we might become murderers just by using our tongues. When we cast words of damnation and misfortune, we instill sadness, anguish and death. Maybe you have been the victim and not the author of such badly said words. How do we get rid of this evil, how do we get out of this pattern? If the words you have heard were along these lines:

"You are useless, you are a failure, nothing you do will ever work. You will never be someone"...

You should verbally dispel out loud all these claims and at the same time announce loud and clear the very opposite of these words. Do that with conviction, even if you are having doubts inside your heart, do not give up, do not look back. Believe in everything you are saying and live the same way. Believe, it is truly possible to turn the tables. Dare to break this vicious cycle of misfortune, bitterness and loneliness.

You can write a new story. All you need to do is to be thankful for what you already have, live consciously, to do everything with excellence and then what you need will get to you! Believe. Do not doubt yourself and you will achieve it!

The spirituality preserves Body and Mind

Studies have shown that people that are grateful for what they have, like good health, family, work and friends are healthier and can rely on more stable and loving relationships. Numerous researches have also attested that the more spiritualized we are, less health issues we are going to develop. Faith can help us stabilize our blood pressure, strengthening our immune system, reducing the risk of cancer and heart diseases. Children who grow up with parents that keep this lifestyle are muchmore confident, less likely to develop bad friendships, and less prone to consume drugs and excessive alcohol.

The Power of Gratitude

Be grateful, instead of grumbling. I encourage you to sing and say thanks. Develop "the good eye", thus being able to see the wonderful things happening around you, while also being grateful for what you already have.

Start your day being grateful. Say thanks for your life, for your sound health, for your family, for your work, and for your relationships. Also say thanks for the things still to come. Say thanks today. Say thanks every day.

Gratefulness makes your fears go away, flourishing abundance.

Personal analysis

1. Answer sincerely: Are you normally grateful or unappreciative? In what way has this attitude been impacting your life?

____

____

____

2. If you've noticed you can improve, I will leave you a guide with some simple questions that will make you reflect, thus helping you to build an easy guide on how to start showing your gratitude.

QUESTIONING	ANSWER	HOW WILL I MANIFEST MY GRATITUDE?
Who is the person that is always ready to listen and to help me when I need?		
In the last few days, has there been anyone who did something that made you proud and happy?		
What has life given you that you have been wishing for some time?		
Who is the person who has constantly encouraged and motivated you to be someone better helping you to reach this moment of growth?		

Who is the person that makes you laugh the most?		
Who is the person that makes you feel loved the most?		
What goals have you achieved this last year?		
What small things are you grateful for?		
What have you learned from a tough moment you have had recently?		
Who are the essential people you are grateful for having in your life?		
What has made you proud of yourself lately?		

Task

Just for today:

Say thanks for everything and for everyone!

Thoughts for meditation

*"Gratitude unlocks the fullness of life.
It turns what we have into enough, and more.
It turns denial into acceptance, chaos into order,
confusion into clarity... It turns a meal into a feast,
a house into a home, a stranger into a friend.
Gratitude makes sense of our past, brings peace
for today and creates a vision for tomorrow."*

Melody Beattie

American writer.

*"A grateful person is loyal, reliable, and will always
be there for you. It is someone you can always trust.
An ungrateful person tends to be selfish, treacherous,
Individualistic and their only true friend is themselves."*

Augusto Branco

Brazilian writer and poet.

"You've got to sing like you don't need the money, love like you'll never get hurt. You've got to dance like no one is watching. It's gotta come from the heart if you want it to work."

Susannah Clark

American painter and songwriter.

"Less is more and more is less."

Psalms 37:16[1]

---

1. https://www.biblestudytools.com/msg/psalms/37.

Chapter 4

SOMETIMES, IT IS GOOD TO BE A CHAMELEON!

"Progress is impossible without change; and those who cannot change their minds cannot change anything."

George Bernard Shaw

4

Everything is constantly changing. The seasons, nature and its colors, months, things and people. Some people, I mean.

Changing is not easy for everyone. Changes generally occur due to adaptation or evolution, thus ensuring survival, and that is a good thing. Those who refuse to change, will die. They will not survive. They will not evolve. According to Leon C. Megginson, it is neither the strongest who are fit for survival, nor the smartest ones, but those who can adapt to changes.[1]

Flexible people are those who easily change to adapt to different situations, having developed the ability to see the positive aspects of transformation. They understand developing patience and steadiness in moments of change is really the best alternative.

Confucius said only the extremely wise and the extremely stupid will not change.[2] We need to develop this emotional skill and try not to be so affected when things do not go as planned. Obviously, everything has its limits, and we can't just let everyone have their way. It is not about being passive either, on the contrary, it is about carefully finding the healthy balance

---

1. WeAreBrain.com. Adaptability: When change is the only constant. Available at:<https://www.wearebrain.com/blog/our-company/adaptability-when-change-is-the-only-constant/> Accessed August 2020.

2. COSTA. J. J.. A sabedoria dos Ditados Populares [The Wisdom of Popular Sayings]. São Paulo: Butterfly, 2009.

to face the crisis, to avoid being devoured by this dark abyss the situation brings.

When we look for the best way to act, for the assertive decision, doing so in a rational and smart way, we become a chameleon, not only ensuring our survival, but also the continuation of life in all its wholesomeness. Stephen Hawking is a perfect example of a "chameleon". He overcame all obstacles life has imposed upon him, choosing not to be limited by them, refusing to complain about his life - "Intelligence is the ability to adapt to change"[1], he once said.

...the bamboo, no matter how much it bends, will always remain a bamboo.

Flexibility: one of the keys of leadership

Flexibility is the ability to give in without breaking by being resilient enough to bend and not crack. The bamboo is an excellent example of resilience, and therefore it is used to make fishing rods. When it needs to bend, it has no trouble doing so, but after a while, it will easily return to its natural state. This means the bamboo, no matter how much it bends, will always remain a bamboo.

Inflexible people hardly give in because they turn any situation into a personal matter as if negative things were personally confronting them, and instead of yielding, they become even stiffer, bad mood

---

1. Extracted from the article: "Intelligence is the ability to adapt to change" — Stephen Hawking's impact on the disabled culture and the people. Available at:<https://medium.com/arise-impact/intelligence-is-the-ability-to-adapt-to-change-stephen-hawkings-impact-on-the-disabled-culture-6668e97caa6b>. Accessed August 2020.

kicks in, harsh inconvenient words may be said and tensions grow even stronger and all that may ultimately be their doom. They have a hard time compromising because, unconsciously or not, they believe they will lose their essence, they will stop being who they are.

The flexibility skills of the "bamboo people" reveal a great deal of maturity and emotional intelligence because they understand that when they give in, they will not stop being themselves. Being flexible, learning how to see through someone else's eyes, trying to understand how someone feels is an incredible trait of strong and extraordinary people.

The Chameleon and the Dragon

Chameleons are amazing animals, of singular beauty, they possess many skills that go way beyond the camouflage we all know so well. They can adapt to any situation. They may live either in a tropical forest or in a scalding desert. In order to adapt and to resist such sharp changes, you need to be tough. This is not for those who are constantly moaning about their lives - according to my upbringing roots, we compare in Portuguese the chuckling of the Angola hens to moaning. This chuckling would be an onomatopoeia similar to "I'm weak, I'm weak".

Adapting, being flexible in face of many challenges that your life may bring you obviously is not for just anyone out there. This includes resolve, yes; I honestly believe developing this ability depends exclusively on what I decide to be and to live.

If I see myself as a poor thing, feeling like a victim of everyone or everything, all I am doing in this life is complaining and regretting. I will live a miserable life. I will blame everyone around me and I will die without having lived my life to the fullest. Weak people do that. Weak people have a weak and shallow life. Superficial relationships, shallow moments of enthusiasm and joy; weak in sense and purpose. See, life is what you choose to be: strong or weak.

Chameleons not only can change their colors, blending in with the environment for protection, but they also do so as a means of communication. Sometimes, we need to yield in some aspect to establish an effective communication whether in professional or personal relationships. We may compare this ability to immerse in your surroundings to the ability of dealing with anyone or any kind of situation. Finding this balance, while avoiding putting yourself on the spotlight and avoiding making a scene, is a highly valuable thing.

In dangerous or life threatening situations, the chameleon can stay completely still and quickly adapt to the environment in a way not to be noticed. It may be boiling from inside but on the outside it displays unshakeable serenity. Unlike some people we know, right?

Weak people have a weak, shallow life. Shallow relationships, shallow moments of enthusiasm and joy; shallow in sense and purpose.

Another interesting ability the chameleon has is its 360-degree view and what is more astonishing, in addition to this, it can even focus on two directions at once - all of this at the same time. It is something truly remarkable, its eyes can move separately, and so, each eye can focus on different objects or situations, thus providing two different points of view. They literally have their other eye up the chimney. This ability to see things from all angles, to see two sides of a coin may allow us to adequately ponder any situation. When we do not fixate our eyes only on the negative part of the story, but rather analyze all points, trying to find the positive side too, we find balance and flexibility more easily.

Oh! Chameleons can also see ultraviolet light and if exposed to this light their social activity increases as well as their reproductive and feeding efficiency. Even in the darkest moments of life they find a way to become better.

What a lesson!

Mahatma Gandhi advised us to let nature teach us and see how it works continually and in silence.[1]

What pearls of wisdom!

Having good communication and expression skills is an excellent thing but during the crisis it is best to keep your mouth shut, you should only say what is worth being repeated later.

Flexibility is also a synonymous with confidence. Flexible people trust life and they know everything will be fine so they will pass this confidence to others. It is amazing how well we feel around

When we do not fixate our eyes only on the negative part of the story, but rather analyze all points, trying to find the positive side too, we find balance and flexibility more easily.

---

1. Covey, Stephen R., and James C. Collins. The 7 habits of highly effective people: powerful lessons in personal change. New York, NY:
Simon & Schuster, 2013.

people like that, no matter what we are going through. Consequently, it is fair to admit that... "chameleon" people are quite different from their "dragon cousins", which lack the same flexibility and tend to breathe fire through their noses.

Dragons make the environment around them awfully heavy because they usually complain about everything and get annoyed over the simplest things. Worst of all, dragons hardly realize how much of an inconvenience they are. Making life hard is an easy task because life is not easy by nature, the hardest thing is to make it lighter, more enjoyable. So, now I ask you:

...during the crisis, it is best to keep your mouth shut, you should only say what is worth being repeated later.

"What are you: a chameleon or a dragon?"

The change that leads to growth

According to Dan Millman[1], every positive change - every leap to a higher level of energy and consciousness - involves a rite of passage. For every step into a higher position on our personal evolution, we must go through a period of initiation and discomfort.

In fact, there is no exception when it comes to natural and consistent growth. It will hurt because old patterns need to be broken for new patterns to rise. This kind of change will only be

---

1. QUODID. Available at: http://quodid.com/quotes/10572/dan-millman/every-positive-
-change-every-jump-to-a. Accessed August 2020.

available when we throw away our old shells. What you need to understand is that the old must leave so the new can come up.

A Sacred Being

For many African tribes, the chameleon is considered a sacred animal. It is quite rare and hard to find. It has its mind and body ready to go through adversities and to adapt to change. Similarly, people with these abilities are extremely rare, unfortunately, even harder to find. They have deep wisdom, they trust themselves and their lives and because of this they also have something to teach in every situation.

So, my dear, make a decision to be part of this rare group of extraordinary people and make the difference around you, choosing to bring balance and peace into the chaos of this world, to those around you and to yourself.

.

Personal analysis

1. How do you react to adversities?

____

____

____

2. Are you more like a chameleon or a dragon? Why?

____

____

____

3. What personal traits do you NEED to the develop from now on to have a better life?

____

____

____

4. TRY TO THINK IN A PRACTICAL WAY and WRITE on how you are going to achieve this:

____

____

____

____

Task

1. When a crisis approaches, be the chameleon, not the dragon.

Do not burst into flames, this is not good for your mental and physical health.

In an ongoing crisis, if we are not flexible, we may end up saying horrible things which we may regret bitterly later but unfortunately it may be already too late. Do not cry over spilled milk. Simply do not spill it. It is that simple.

2. Be clever and focus on positive thoughts and good vibrations to beat the crisis at hand.

3. Develop the 360-degree arc of view. Everything has a good and a bad side. Choose to give more attention to the positive side instead of cultivating grumbling.

4. Do not react, act. Have a positive attitude and make a difference. Be the example of steadiness among chaos.

5. Learn to adapt, be quiet and wait. The storm will go away and life will go on.

Do not be afraid.

6. Get mentally and physically ready to adapt and change during troubling times; avoid freaking out or throwing a fit. This is not suited for mature and emotionally intelligent people.

7. In moments of crisis, do not murmur, say thanks.

Do not fall apart, instead get stronger.

Thoughts for meditation

*"No matter how far you went
the wrong way. Turn back."*

Turkish Proverb

*"All inner reform and all change for the better depend
exclusively on the application of our own effort."*

Immanuel Kant

German philosopher and founder of
Critical Philosoph.

"You must be the change you wish to see in the world."

Mahatma Gandhi

Pacifist leader, Idealizer and founder
of the modern Indian State.

*"The world hates change, yet it is the
only thing that has brought progress."*

Charles F. Kettering

American inventor and engineer, founder
of Delco and author of 186 patent.

*"When the winds of change lob, some
people build obstacles, others build windmills."*

Érico Veríssimo

Brazilian writer of the Second
Phase of Modernism.

Chapter 5

GRAB THE PEN!

"It had long since come to my attention that people of accomplishment rarely sat back and let things happen to them. They went out and happened to things."

Elinor Smith (1911 - 2010)

Pioneering American aviator also the youngest licensed pilot in the world at 16.

5

L et's be honest: it is hard to grab a pen and write our own story. It is a quest we are in since the dawn of our lives. Even as children, we have the need to please our parents. Even if it dismays us, we want to do their bidding. We try, although unconsciously, to respect their will. When a child behaves like expected and follows a certain pattern they get into a comfortable position,their image before their parents will be positive and this will make them feel good. However, deep inside, they might not feel complete or even happy with themselves.

Time passes and we grow up but this infant remains with us and unconsciously we keep trying to please important people in our lives, for several reasons, trying to behave the right way to get attention or even feel accepted. I am not saying there is something wrong with it as children. On the contrary, our identity and personality are being formed and we need to be guided by limits, rules and "compasses" that will point out what we should do or how we should proceed. However, **it stops being a healthy thing when, after fully grown, we are not able to make our own decisions based on our values, dreams and aspirations, when we are unable to be faithful to these principles** because of what people around us think.

Take the Lead Role

Being the main character of your own story is literally using the pen. It is making your decisions and being responsible for them. This expression "using the pen" is normally used when we refer to people who have the authority and power to change the destiny of a person, a company, a city or a country, someone with power to give a verdict. I like the principle that we must honor the authorities and I firmly believe in it, but just as a judge can only pass a sentence in a specific case there are decisions in our lives only we can make. A simple example: your college major. It is sad, but we have seen many cases of young students fulfilling their parents' wishes as they go to college. They are studying to be a lawyer, a doctor, an engineer or any other career not by choice, but because their parents told them to. Later they will have to pursue a job their parents chose for them and in the long run maybe, the disappointments are so many that life itself begins to lose meaning.

A failed life is certainly the one we live to please others.

Be attentive to what you like, what is important in your life and learn to hear your inner voice, being faithful to it. Your inner voice will not fail. A messed up life, no shadow of a doubt, is one we live to please others. Let me repeat this, a failed life is built by actions and choices based on pleasing others.

When this happens, it does not take long for the frustrations to seize our emotions, thoughts, and finally our actions. Then our actions will be different from our values and this will enhance our sensation of dissatisfaction or even frustration.

Master the Art of Saying: "No"!

If we want to truly be a main character in our own story, we need to master the art of saying no. Some people have a great deal of trouble saying no to other's requests and even if they suffer because of it, they will not respect their desires and longings, maybe they will not express their own opinions. **See, having a hard time saying no is usually related to low self-esteem**.

If I do not do what others ask me out of fear, I may put in jeopardy the admiration they have for me. If this idea of "they may not like me anymore" becomes unbearable, then I will give in more and more, corrupting myself. I sabotage myself by not being faithful to my own conceptions, to what I really like or believe, to what I really want, believe or intent to do. I will start giving in, betraying my ethical values and morality deceiving my own self.

To conquer this, there is only one way: I need to learn how to love myself which we will see deeper later on and understand that **my value is not based on the way I please others, even less on what people think of me**.

An Unexplored Richness

´Know thyself´ and so understand and learn how to truly respect yourself. We may end up provoking irreversible damage to our lives if we do not get to know ourselves. Seek this treasure. Solomon once said, knowledge is more valuable than any treasure, more precious than gold and silver. Explore the richness of knowing deeply who you are.

You are a gold mine, a precious diamond. Self-knowledge will help you polish what is needed and then you will shine, revealing your true light and fulfilling your purpose, your real mission on this planet.

I dare you to take the pen of your life and write your own story. Choose to live what you have always dreamed of, fight for it, believe it and dare to pay the price. Seek, conquer, do not look back, decide not to hear those negative voices and criticisms preventing you from moving forward, until now.

I admit the path may not be easy but it is the only way to bring you the satisfaction of fighting and winning. Do not pay attention to what others think. Dare to live your own life and enjoy it as much as possible, developing your potential with excellence and leave your mark, your legacy in the history of mankind...

Personal analysis

1. From 0 to 10, how much do you know yourself?

____

____

____

2. If you gave yourself a bad grade, what will you do to change this situation?

____

____

____

3. From 0 to 10, how much your actions have been in accordance with your dreams?

____

____

____

4. Make a short list of practical things you need to make your dreams come true.

____

____

____

____

5. To "make it happen", you will probably need to develop some traits or skills. Which skills are those and what do I need to do to improve them?

____

____

____

____

____

____

____

____

____

Task

1. In the next few days, try to become aware of the following situations:

a) Do you do what others expect you to do even if it goes against your schedule or against your previously established purpose?

(   ) Yes   (   ) No   (   ) Sometimes.

b) How do you behave when you feel like saying no? Pay attention to how your body reacts, how you usually answer and then how you feel about yourself and about what happened. Write it down here. This will help develop your self-knowledge.

____

____

____

____

c) Try to understand why you act like that. If you identify your limiting thoughts, you will gradually be more aware of your shortcomings. Watch yourself instead and try to notice this: which thoughts go through your mind during this moment that leads to self-sabotage? Put them down.

____

____

____

2. Once you identify what your source point is, what is preventing you from being the main character, inevitably strength will start growing from within as you recognize your weaknesses. You will be aware of the triggers that make you fall.

In that case, you will have to fight these triggers back. Try and understand that the battle is not against yourself or other people. Your victory will come from changing the way you think about yourself. As to illustrate, when you yield, get frustrated and angry at yourself for doing what you don't want and end up considering: "how can you be so dumb? When will you stop being such an idiot?"

This is extremely aggressive, using the kind of words you don't even dare saying to the people you love, so how can we treat ourselves like that without undermining our self-esteem and destroying our self-confidence?

However, if you do this in a gentle way, maybe saying something like:

"(Say your name)... I am sorry I was not loyal to you. Forgive me. I will not do this to you again. Your opinion deserves to be respected and heard. Forgive me. I love you".

Does it sound strange speaking to yourself in this manner? Haha, well, it is, but this is a reason to cry and not to laugh. It is evidence of the type of the self-love relationship we have. If we cannot treat ourselves with the due respect and care, we should not be surprised when others do not do it either...

3. Write in a little poster the traits you need to develop to become the main character, the person in charge of your story and put

it somewhere you get to see often and leave it for as long as you may, even when those traits become part of your life. Write them as if they were part of you already. If you want, you may use the meditation I have elaborated down here to help you as an example, adding what you wish with your own words. Practice the following meditation as much as you can within the next 21 days (next page). Do this meditation right after you wake up and before you go to bed.

Meditation: Forging a main character

*I am a strong, brave and determined person. I am loyal to my
principles and values. If I must, I easily say no because I know who
I am. This way, I am not shaken by what others think, I understand
now I cannot please everyone without harming myself, my values
and priorities I have already set.*

*I have the right to live my life.
I have the right to make my decisions based on my dreams, my
principles and values. There is no problem saying "no" because
I have the right to be loyal with me, the right not to boycott myself,
staying strong in this path to achieve my dreams and
fulfill my purpose.*

*I do not need others' approval
to feel like a unique, validated and loved person.
I pray " the Eternal" guides me every day towards the purest
light so I may fulfill my purpose here on Earth; may nothing divert
me from accomplishing His incredible project for me.
Gratitude.
Amen.*

Thoughts for meditation

*"Accept no one's definition of your
life but define yourself."*

Harvey Firestone

American entrepreneur, founder of Firestone,
a company that was the biggest producer of pneumatic
components in the USA during the eighties.

*"Your time is limited so don't
waste it living someone else's life."*

Steve Jobs

American inventor and entrepreneur.
He was the co-founder, CEO, executive director
of Apple Inc. and stood out for having
revolutionized six industrial branches: personal
computers, animation movies, music, telephones,
tablets, and digital publications.

*"Learn to say no; it will be of more
use to you than to be able to read Latin."*

Charles Spurgeon (1834-1892)

English writer and Baptist preacher,
considered the Prince of Preachers.

"The best way to predict the future is to create it."

Peter Drucker

Austrian writer, considered the father
of modern management.

"Each man must invent his own path."

Jean-Paul Sartre

French writer and philosopher, one of the
key figures in the philosophy of existentia.

Chapter 6

TRY TO REACH THE MOON

"

"Let us strive for the impossible. The great achievements throughout history have been the conquest of what seemed impossible."

Charles Chaplin (1889 - 1977)

British actor of the silent era of movies, director, songwriter, playwright, producer and editor.

6

Dreams do not think, do not articulate, do not go to work. Only you can make dreams happen. A dream will never stop being a dream unless you do something about it. Doing something means choosing. Choosing comes from priorities and priorities are limited by how much you let go of other things. It is not easy. By the way, reaching the moon has never been that easy. Achieving your dreams, I AM SORRY TO TELL YOU, is something outside of your comfort zone.

To reach your dream, you must act. You need to take the first step, even if the "journey" scares you. Dreams are not handed on a beautiful plate by a delivery service straight to your home. Martin Luther King Jr. once said, "Achieved dreams are the result of several combined actions". You need to plan your strategies. Set a plan of action and execute it. MOVE YOURSELF! There is an old Portuguese saying "past waters do not move the mill".

You are an unlimited soul thus your potential for growth.

We need to set high standards for ourselves. You are an unlimited soul thus your potential for growth.

"I am moving away from everything that hinders me, that deceives me, that holds me back, that restrains me. I am getting closer to anything that makes me whole, makes me happy and wishes me well".[1]

What hinders you?

This line of thought, "I'll say it tomorrow, I'll do it tomorrow" has kept thousands of people from living their dreams. Why? Because there was no tomorrow for them. Postponing things is a problem for many people.

What is hindering you? Do you think you are going to live forever? Wake up!!! In fact, you only have today. The now is the only thing you can rely on, so stop delaying what could be done today. Try to understand that you do not really have a tomorrow.

If you knew you would die today, what would you try to finish before your time expired? Do you realize how your priorities would change then? **How many times do we prioritize what is URGENT instead of what is IMPORTANT?** The problem is this becomes a usual thing in our daily routines. We are now living for what is urgent, leaving aside what is really important, there is where danger lies and saying I'LL DO IT TOMORROW, I'LL SAY IT TOMORROW is a trivial thing nowadays. Don't leave for tomorrow what you can do today. There will be other distractions just as there are distractions today. Don't postpone anymore and make the change today. Every day counts! Since tomorrow death may knock at your door, sickness

---

1. Caio Fernando Abreu, a Brazilian writer and playwright, Who has brilliantly given us these great tips to reach the moon.

may come, divorce may happen, your children spread their wings and eventually tomorrow IS TOO LATE.

What deceives you?

"The heart is deceitful above all things. "

Jeremiah 17:9

The heart is the center of our emotions. Our emotions emerge and are validated by our thoughts and despite the fact they appear to be true to us, our thoughts may be quite wrong and misleading. Thoughts such as "well, to make it work, I should have been born in another family, have had another upbringing, have found support and encouragement..."

You know, I truly believe we are the main character of our lives and no matter the circumstances around us, we can break the shackles of thoughts and emotions that cast us as the victims in our own stories.

What holds you back?

Sorrow? Resentments over what others have not done for you?

This "poor little thing syndrome" holds us back, preventing us from growing, making it impossible to develop our potential. Think about it...

What restrains you?

Lacking courage? We need to be strong to expose our weaknesses, right? The fear of taking risks, of being exposed to criticism, of hearing many things we do not like... Please understand once and for all, we will never be ready.

Do not be restrained for not feeling fully ready to accomplish what you want; this is coward!

Be bold and brave, always move forward!

Stop hesitating, stop walking around in circles.

Climb that mountain, break free from your own limitations, take the risk and live your dreams!

Nothing comes free!

It is true! Everything has a price. Nothing is sadder than ending your journey without having achieved what you wanted the most and not because you could not reach it, merely because you simply did not have the courage to try.

Notable men and women, who left remarkable contributions, had to try several times to reach the moon. Among them, Abraham Lincoln, Thomas Edison, Nelson Mandela, Steve Jobs, Oprah and so many others. They did not reach it neither on the first attempt nor on the second one. The most shocking fact is that some of them could not reach it even on the hundredth attempt.

Then I ask you, how many times are you willing to try to reach the moon?

You deserve to give yourself this chance!

Mistakes are part of the process

If you fail on your first try, do not give up! If you fail on the second try, be persistent! If you also fail on the third try, you should go on! Remember, we learn more from our apparent failures than from our victories!

Do not look back! Each step ahead is a step closer to your goal and only by reaching it you will be worthy of your prize!

You cannot afford to stop if you have not reached the moon yet. This is what we call PERSEVERANCE! We will talk about it in another chapter. The main thing now is making you understand that what you want is achievable.

Put yourself together!

Take responsibility over things that have happened in your life. Maturity is not about blaming others for your failures but rather, learning from them and understanding that our losses and gains are an immediate consequence of our thoughts and actions.

When you take responsibility, not only you show you are mature, but you also grow with the lessons life gives you, even if they come from the most tragic and saddest moments of your existence.

If you want to achieve your dreams, I encourage you to set as your objective:

MOVE FORWARD instead of focusing on frustrations. Progressing demands focus and determination. Do not stop pushing ahead because someone you expected support from was not there, or they even criticized you. Stop right now with any kind of grumbling or mumbling and get your act together, set clear target, and try to understand:

YOU AND ONLY YOU, ARE RESPONSIBLE FOR REACHING YOUR GOALS!

Go to work!

If you, like me, want to reach the moon, roll up your sleeves, get off the sofa and "don't miss the bus".[1]

To reach the moon you must be a giant. A giant in attitude for only wanting something is pointless, just wishing something does not get anyone anywhere. Everyone wants to be successful, rich, healthy, travel around the world and have a good life, however, only a few will truly pursue these things. Why? Because wanting something is not enough. What changes the story is your ATTITUDE!

Mahatma Gandhi, leader of the Indian Independence Movement, once said, "You may never know what results come of your actions, but if you do nothing, there will be no results". This way, you must be mentally ready for all adversities and remember:

---

1. Vai trabalhar Vagabundo! Chico Buarque's Song, Brazilian singer and songwriter. Available at https://genius.com/Chico-buarque-vai-trabalhar-vagabundo-annotated. Accessed August 2020.

Organization, Focus, Determination, Responsibility and Attitude are the main ingredients to reach the moon and get everything else you want!

Keep in mind that if you follow the steps above the impossible becomes possible, something you can touch, feel and live!

Personal analysis

1. The biggest trait of winners is choosing not to be a victim of adverse situations. Do a thorough analysis and answer honestly: Do I tend to victimize myself, blaming others or my own story?

____

____

____

____

2. If your answer is yes, congratulations on your honesty.

Recognizing your weaknesses is the first step to change.

From now on, refuse to be a victim, no matter what others do or say to you. Remember that playing the victim may stray you from achieving your dreams and live your life to the fullest. So, promptly refuse any victimizing thoughts, abandon completely and ultimately "this poor little thing syndrome". What thoughts are boycotting you that you should let go?

____

____

____

Task

1. What areas have you noticed you are not so mature and yet, you will be more responsible and aware from now on?

____

____

____

2. How do you plan on putting this into practice?

____

____

____

3. How do you react in critical moments and how would you wish to behave next time?

____

____

____

4. Now I ask you: "Will you or will you not try to reach the moon?"

Leave your comfort zone and fight for your dreams. I guarantee you this: nothing will drops out of the sky! Usually, what drops out of there may be trouble for those on the ground. Think about it! Big achievements come with lots of effort, work and willfulness. It is important to say "It is possible, I will achieve it, I will live the unachievable!"

5. Given this, I ask you, which dreams have you deemed to be difficult or even impossible to achieve?

____

____

____

6. Which aspects do I need to develop to achieve:

( ) discipline
( ) motivation
( ) getting out of the comfort zone
( ) believing

Personal Considerations:

Thoughts for meditation

*"A dream will never stop being
a dream unless you act about it.
Whatever you can do or dream
you can have, just begin it.
Boldness has genius, power
and magic in it."*

Johann Goethe (1749 - 1832)

One of the key figures of German literature
and European Romanticism.

*"Dreaming the impossible is the
first step to make it possible."*

Confúcio (551 - 479 A.C.)

Chinese philosopher and thinker.

"The future belongs to those who believe in the beauty of their dreams."

Eleanor Roosevelt (1884-1962)

American First Lady. Advocate
for Human Rights.

"We have to dream, because if we don't, things won't happen."

Oscar Niemeyer (1907 - 2012)

Brazilian architect, a key figure
to modern architecture.

"If you can dream, you can do it."

Walt Disney (1901 - 1966)

Film producer and co-founder
of Walt Disney Company.

Chapter 7

EYES ONTO THE TARGET

*"Talent hits a target no one else can hit;
Genius hits a target no one else can see."*

Arthur Schopenhauer (1788 - 1860)

19th century German philosopher.

What targets do you want to hit in your life? What objectives have you set to reach them?

Once I asked this very question to someone who then answered back:

"I have no objectives, nor targets, nor dreams. I don't plan ahead anything because if I plan, dream and try to program something in my life, it will all go wrong."

This person had a firm conviction there was no point setting goals to achieve in life. No point in planning, focusing or even bother dreaming because failure would meet them at a faster pace. If that is true, any path would be good then. But if we have such an attitude, then we cannot complain afterwards where we end up or what we ultimately achieve.

What do you want?

Even before anything, before even talking about focus, you need to know what you want for your life.

Seriously, if you do not know what you want, there is no reason talking about focus, because you can only get a good shot if you have something to aim for.

Reflecting Now

Reflect carefully and answer the questions below:

1. What do you want, really?

____

____

____

2. What do you want for your love life?

____

____

____

3. For your relationships? Family, friends, colleagues...?

____

____

____

4. For your career?

____

____

____

5. How are you spending your life? What are you investing your days on?

____

____

____

____

6. Is it paying off?

____

____

____

____

7. Is this really what you want?

____

____

____

____

8. What makes you happy at the end of the day?

____

____

____

____

9. Bearing in mind all this analysis, reflect about this last question: why do you want that all?

____

____

____

Enough questions for now, I promise.

Why knowing the 'whys' is so important

I know this exercise wasn't easy, nevertheless it is essential to understand **what we want and why we want it**, because we shouldn't want something just to prove to others we can make it, to show our worth or that we are in fact 'mister' someone but, simply because we want it and this will make all the difference.

When you want something and you know why you want it, something amazing happens: that thing will become your life, your universe. You will be immersed in this new world and your focus will be automatic, the result of your aspirations will become a consequence of your own wish and persistence. However if you do not know what you want,

Being overwhelmed does not leave you room for excellence.

you will look at a thousand things, so you may be absorbed by many other things and then not much goes on, because you are going to be overloaded. This surely generates a problem. Being overwhelmed does not leave you room for excellence.

But I have some good news: your life will graciously flow if you know what you want and where you want to go. This will make you exercise your focus and constancy daily, developing your skills.

Briefly, know what you want, set your focus, and do not blink your eyes until you reach the target.

The Treasure Map

If I want to earn something valuable in this life, first I must study the treasure map and set the path, should I want to find the treasures I seek. I need to create strategies, to make plans and to determine the time needed for every step, the right moment for every action. This way, I will walk straight to the target and distractions will not divert me from the path, nor will make me stop. I will march on, with my eyes set on the main intent.

If anything attracks, anything distracts. If this is the way I work things out, too little will I accomplish. Therefore, it is so important to think the right way, believing and betting on yourself.

Turkey Shoot

Focus on your target, determination and actions will make all the difference.

So, set to yourself the following objective:

I WILL NOT STOP UNTIL I GET THERE!

Get it? You cannot afford to stop until you have reached it. Some people stop along the way to weep, to complain, to lick their wounds. Be sure that if they ever get there, it will take a long time...

Also set this as a target for yourself:

I WILL DO MY BEST!

Believe me, the rest will come, and before you know, all your dreams will come true. In fact, all you need is having faith.

Do not look back. Why should your dream be surreal if it can be real? Finally, try to understand that only you can make it happen. Others cannot hit your target for you.

The Big Secret

Success is only possible when you are fully involved. This takes self-giving.

If you want achievements, you need to fully dedicate yourself. An obstinate and absolute surrender. This is the big secret of those who kept their focus on their targets, those who have reached what they wanted, they gave every bit of themselves to their dreams, they worked really hard to achieve their goals, and renounced everything to live it. We want to live incredible things, we want to achieve almost impossible dreams but, what have we given for that? In what ways have we used our time, have we really absolutely compromised ourselves to this quest? How much have we dedicated ourselves to perform this task?

The Power of Engagement

When I have something to focus on in my life and I am committed to it, this engagement will not only lead me to where I want, but it will also bring great satisfaction, because I see evolution. There is constant development simply because there is deliberate engagement. This development brings joy and it is a fundamental part of happiness in our lives. Because truthfully, what really matters is not success (which is measured by others) however, the fulfillment

I develop during my lifetime (which is my view of my own existence). What I have done, where I came from, what I have overcome, what I have achieved. All of this is the basis for the person I am and how I see myself.

So, you should be aware of the importance of knowing what you want,being focused on it and ultimately accomplishing it. This is the foundation of your path and it will give meaning to your existence, because you are not what you have, but the legacy you leave. You are the memories you carve on people's hearts. It is something totally in tune with your essence which in turn, reverberates what you want and where you look at, this is what your FOCUS is.

...there is constant development, simply because there is deliberate engagement.

Task

1. Write down your objectives. Define strategies and split them into smaller steps you will need to take, in a wise order.

____

____

____

____

____

____

____

____

2. Once the steps are set, give them a proper deadline. Be strict with yourself.

If needed, share this with someone close. Someone who will stimulate you and motivate you along the way and who will not allow you to keep complaining about how hard things are instead.

3. Follow the journey you planned religiously, giving yourself a reward for every step you have reached. Rejoice at every task completed, celebrating every minor triumph, because **small victories lead to the final victory**.

Thoughts for meditation

"You can't depend on your eyes when your imagination is out of focus."

Mark Twain (1835 - 1910)

American writer and humorist,
critic of racism.

"People think focus means saying yes to the thing you've got to focus on. But that's not what it means at all. It means saying no to the hundred other good ideas that there are. You have to pick carefully."

Steve Jobs (1955 - 2011)

American Inventor, Businessman,
and Information technology tycoon.

*"You must remain focused on
your journey to greatness."*

Les Brown (1945 -   )

American motivational speaker.

*"Without dreams, life has no glow.
Without goals, dreams have no foundation.
Without priorities, dreams don't become real.
Dream, set goals and priorities, take risks
to make your dreams true.
It is best to make a mistake by trying
than to make a mistake by omission."*

Augusto Cury (1958 -   )

Brazilian psychiatrist, professor, and writer.
Author of The Multifocal Intelligence Theory.

*"If you want to be successful,
you need full dedication,
you have to find your last
limit and give your best."*

Ayrton Senna (1960 - 1994)

Brazilian F1 driver, three-time.
world champion in 1988, 1990, and 1991.

"One man is no more than another,
if he does no more than what another does."

Miguel de Cervantes (1547 - 1616)

Spanish poet, novelist, and playwright.
His masterpiece was Don Quixote.

Chapter 8

YOU MUST PERSEVERE!

"

*"The first steps are useless if you
don't go all the way."*

Adi Shankara (788 - 820 a.C.)

Indian philosopher and theologian.

W hat price am I willing to pay?

When you really want to achieve something, you will do anything for it. Obstinate people will find a way, a path, they will create the opportunity, the formula and turn impossible things into possible. They bend over backwards, as it is commonly said. Others are not so perseverant, so they come up with excuses.

Thomas Edison is a fine example of perseverance, as he once said, "I have not failed. I have just found 10,000 ways that will not work." He emphasized how we should not give up in face of our mistakes, but instead learn a lesson from them, and keep trying until we reach our goal.

The only difference between failure and triumph is perseverance. Many times, we look at what we want and say: "It is very hard, I will not succeed".

The root of the problem

We put ourselves in a dilemma when we believe this idea of "I'm not going to make it; it is too much for me", so we end up backing down before we even try. Do not do that!

If the path seems too long, split it in smaller segments and take the first step! A long journey is made little by little. Pay attention, be mindful of that, you must go step-by-step. Some people want to achieve things by simply galloping towards their objective, they have no respect for the stages of development we all must go through. That is why they give up. They blame others, saying they did not even have a chance. That they were misunderstood.

However, almost a 100% of those who achieved their dreams had to endure a long, extenuating way, without looking back.

So, take the first step and then the second, do not pay attention to the thirtieth or the hundredth step right now and do not look back either, take one step at a time, this way you will get out of your comfort zone and even with tiny daily developments, you will already feel stimulated to keep going. Then, switch the "this is impossible" for "just today, I will do everything that is possible".

Extraordinary people do not give up!

Big achievements are not on the list of easy things to be obtained. The truth is, nothing is easy and comes for free. **Epic victories are not engraved on the tombs of those who gave up. In fact, extraordinary people do not give up** at all. They may trip, fall and also fail however they will not stop. They learn from their mistakes and then get up even stronger.

The big riddle of life

You know, I have learned that the biggest riddle in life is what we do in painful times. Pain always changes us. For some, pain helps to be a better person, yet for others, unfortunately, pain makes them worse. You are the one who decides in which ways pain will shape you. You decide into what pain will transform you, someone sweeter or bitter, someone who feels like a loser or goes through pain even more committed to life, passionate about your dreams and focused on building your legacy. So, do not just persevere through difficulties, you should make an effort to grow from them, for pain may be your best friend or your greatest enemy.

There is no escaping, **PAIN WILL ALWAYS CHANGE YOU**. It will either destroy you or turn you into someone much better than before. A piece of advice: who gets to decide the outcome is YOU. It all depends on you. So, keep in mind what you have just learned:

1st Do not give up.

2nd Persevere!

Now, I have some good and bad news. The good news is:

If you choose to persevere, you will grow, you will mature, and you will be honored.

The bad news is, if you want to keep licking your wounds, if you play the victim of your own story, you will reach nowhere and you will probably leave no footprint on this Earth!

I do not believe in victory without pain or achievements without leaving behind the tempting invitation of playing the victim's role. Firmly accept this challenge called Perseverance!

Your life now is your great opportunity. If you cannot see it clearly, then create it, but do not give up!

Perseverance shapes our characters since it fosters patience and constancy. It is about enduring pain to receive later, a reward. This develops maturity!

Your life now is your great opportunity.

Confucius once said wisely, "The man who moves a mountain begins by carrying small stones". Maybe you look at your dreams and see something too big, almost impossible, however, if you persevere and keep working on it, even by taking tiny steps, believe me, you will reach your objective. It may be a long way, but you will get there. I guarantee!

Personal analysis

Reflect for a moment:

1. So far, what is really preventing you from achieving what you want?

____

____

____

2. Do a cautious analysis and ask yourself, "if I were not listening to all the negative talk around me, could I be further along the way?"

____

____

____

3. Thomas Edison was deaf, and instead of playing a victim, he said: "Being deaf was of great help to me. It spared me the trouble of having to listen to the great amount of useless conversations and taught me to hear my inner voice."

In face of such a wise statement, what can you learn from Edison?

____

____

____

____

Task

1. Take the first step.

2. Split your path in smaller steps, goals to be achieved with set deadlines.

3. Persevere.

4. Persevere again.

5. Do not look back.

6. Be deaf to all the discouraging voices.

7. If you lose encouragement along the way, take a look at what you have done already, how much you have developed, pay attention to where you came from and where you are right now. Through this reflection, take a deep breath, realize the winner you already are, pat yourself on the back and proceed even more perseverant than before!

Thoughts for meditation

"Little by little the bird builds its nest."

Popular Saying

"Persistence achieves the impossible."

Chinese Proverb

*"Don't stop, because it will be
the same as turning back."*

Pe. Juan Eusébio Nieremberg (1595 - 1658)

Spanish humanist, physicist, biographer and theologist.

"Genius is one percent inspiration,
ninety-nine percent perspiration.
Our greatest weakness lies in giving up.
The most certain way to succeed is
always to try just one more time."

Thomas Alva Edison (1847-1931)

American Businessman who patented and financed the development of many devices of great importance to the industry. He became known as The Wizard of Menlo Park, one of the first inventors to apply the principles of organized science and teamwork to the process of invention.

"Each dream you leave behind
is a part of your future that will no longer exist."

Steve Jobs (1955-2011)

American Inventor, Businessman, and Information technology tycoon.
He was a co-founder, CEO and executive director of Apple Inc.. He stood out for having revolutionized six industrial branches: personal computers, animation movies, music, telephones, tablets and digital publications.

Chapter 9

ALWAYS LEARNING

"Learning is changing ways."

Plato

He was a philosopher and mathematician from the Classical period of Ancient Greece, author of many philosophical dialogs and founder of the Academy in Athens, the first institution of higher learning in the Western world.

Babies and children are fascinated by one thing: learning. They have this amazing curiosity, they put their finger where they should not, they ask funny questions, they say many unimaginable things, all with the intent of learning. They want to know more and if they do not get satisfying answers, they will not stop asking new questions.

Socrates once said that we learn more from questions than from answers. However, as we grow up, where does our curiosity go? Why does this natural impulse of learning hides itself?

Some are naturally more reserved than others. And yet, it is a natural thing for humans to have this passion for learning, this interest in understanding things and go beyond. Men mastered the fire, then the horses, they made cars, planes and rockets. They went to the moon, even though that was not enough; we always want to know more, understand what is out there, what are the best possibilities in life and this curiosity prevents men from stopping. According to Sigmund Freud, men lose much of their potential when they leave behind this childish trait of being so alive, perceptive and curious. He once pondered, "What a distressing contrast there is between the radiant intelligence of the child and the feeble mentality of the average adult".

We are all born with a radiant intelligence, with a natural and strong desire to learn. Children may even (according to studies) ask hundreds of questions a day and, depending on those surrounding them, they may either be stimulated or discouraged.

The Blessing of Curiosity

*"I have no special talent.
I am only passionately curious."*

Albert Einstein

Seek to kindle this flame of learning in children, teenagers, adults and even elders around you. Especially with children, try to instigate their curiosity by not cutting off their questions.

Everyone needs someone to motivate, inspire them to be better and to seek improvement. Be the flame that lights this passionate fire of learning more. Do not settle for what you already know. Do not dwell on the surface of things. Be curious! Wish to KNOW! And it is not about gaining knowledge just to fill your mind with more information. No! It is **about knowing things with the purpose of becoming someone better; It is about self-love, self-acceptance, being proud of yourself, thus being ready to contribute to a better world.**

The Secret to Learn

If you want your mind to be truly open to learning, you must first open your mind to itself.

Anxiety, depression and other disorders may prevent us from flourishing and may also stop us from getting the best out of life.

To offer our best, to develop our potential and to leave a mark, we need to fully surrender. We need to be completely involved. This way, cultivating thoughts of love, happiness and peace is essential to be ready and open to learn new things. That is why I need to put into practice the '*I love myself*'.[1]

But why learn?

Learn to be better, to grow up not just intellectually, but spiritually and emotionally. We are living in a historical moment of unprecedented technological, scientific and intellectual progress. However, never have we seen so many deaths by suicide and even people not quite at this level of desperation are mostly just existing, not living to the fullest. We are living in a century plagued by an epidemic of depression and anxiety. The W.H.O has predicted that by 2030 Depression will be the most lethal disease, more than Cancer or Heart Conditions.[2]

---

1. Read and practice chapter 14.

2. BBC NEWS. The World Health Organization predicts that within 20 years more people will be affected by depression than any other health problem.

A Hungry Soul

We are living in a time when our most basic desires are easily satisfied. We have comfort and abundant food, nonetheless our souls are starving like they never have.

We have been experiencing a moral and spiritual decadence that results in the collapse of the family and of our principles and values. However, education and virtue are the food of the soul.

What are our souls starved for?

Our souls need solid, sustaining food. Good books, thoughts that elevate our spirit, meditation, prayer, contemplation, and helping someone in their time of need, do good to anyone. This is the daily sustenance our souls require.

We have comfort and abundant food, but our souls are starving like they never were.

So, we should be always learning and the first step to ensure this is being humble. If I just assume that I know everything I need to know, I am being arrogant, then I will be closed for new opportunities and different things to learn.

We were not created to be average, but rather to grow, to intensively develop our potential. Getting the most out of our lives and doing the best we can during our time here, by seeking daily improvement, by accepting no less than excellence. It is not about showing off, it is about being better and greater to serve better.

Serving with excellence, working with primacy and leaving a legacy, bringing hope because, if my reality and also your reality become better, the whole world has already changed a bit.

That is why it is so important not settling for less, instead of it, improving every day. Try to be a better person today than you were yesterday and in the end, you will do the best you can so, you will not have the tragic end of those who live in this terrible zone of conformity, playing as victims, zombies in their own small, self-centered, egocentric world. They live an easily disposable life.

When you improve yourself, you are also showing love to what you are, to what you do and to what you have to offer. Therefore, life becomes your own masterpiece, beautiful and unique, inspiring, shining and contagious.

Personal analysis

1. Have you been feeding your soul? If yes, in what ways?

____

____

____

2. If there is enough quiet within, you may be able to be more perceptive to the needs of your soul. You will clearly notice if it is either satisfied or starving. A disturbed soul is a strong indicator of a state of starvation. A soul in a constant undisturbed, serene, joyful state is a consequence of a spirit that has been daily fed by wise and deep teachings, meditation, prayer and good music.

3. Can you hear your soul asking for food? As we have learned above, this hunger may manifest through anxiety, anguish, sadness, compulsion, and so many other signs your desperate soul will use to let you know if it is starving.

____

____

____

4. I kindly ask you: from now on, take into consideration your soul's needs and take care of it.

Task

1. Learn something new every day;

2. Feed your soul with something uplifting and satisfying. (Good readings, meditation, nature walks, practicing contemplation, developing your spirituality, listening to good music);

3. After your soul has had a good meal, yet, seek to nourish it with a good dessert: do something good to someone. This may be manifested through kind actions, compliments, good advice, donating something, things or even your time;

4. Search for a spiritual community, a place where you feel good, welcome; increase your knowledge and intensify your connection with the Eternal and the eternity that lives in you.

Thoughts for meditation

*"There is a great desire in me to always be better.
It is what makes me happy. Whenever I feel that
I am learning less, that the learning curve
is leveling up, or anything of that sort, I do not feel
so glad about it. And this applies not only
professionally, as a race car driver, but as a person."*

Ayrton Senna (1960 - 1994)

Brazilian F1 driver, three-time world
champion in 1988, 1990 and 1991.

*"I am always doing that which I cannot do,
in order that I may learn how to do it."*

Pablo Picasso (1881 - 1973)

Spanish painter, sculptor, ceramist, set designer, poet,
and playwright who spent most of his life in France.
He is best known as the co-founder of cubism

.

*"In my walks, every man I meet is
my superior in some way and in that,
I learn from him."*

Ralph Waldo Emerson (1803 - 1882)

American writer, philosopher and poet.

*"The best way to be happy
is to contribute to someone's happines."*

Confúcio (551 - 479)

Chinese philosopher and thinker.

Chapter 10

WHAT IF THEY SAY THINGS ABOUT ME?!

*"What Paul Says About Peter Tells Us
More About Paul Than About Peter."*

Baruch Spinoza ((1632-1677)

Dutch Philosopher.

10

Not allowing yourself to get affected by what others are saying or think of you is something that shows deep emotional intelligence.

Some people tend to see themselves through other people's eyes and mouths, so they are moved by compliments or criticism and this behavior puts them in a dangerous ferris wheel. Depending on the stimuli received, an equivalent response is produced. If they are complimented, fine, but if criticized, they will lose their ground.

What miserable life that is, to live guided by what others around me think and say!

It is about maturity

When I am feeling well about myself and about my story, when I love myself and when I accept myself as I am, having forgiven my own flaws and mistakes from the past, and at the same time working hard to be a better person every day, **I will not have any hard time with what people say or think about me**.

So, what is the secret to reaching such maturity?

It is simple: I know who I am.

You may be wondering,

"What do you mean, Jane? Be more specific."

All you need to beat gossip, slanders and innuendos is knowing exactly who you are. This demands self-knowledge and being aligned with your principles and values. Think about it. Yes, because if I live in a consistent way, If I work hard every day to achieve my dreams and goals, if I take care of those I love, If I live as a responsible member of society, why would I get upset about lies that people create to criticize and hinder me?

What to do when people say bad things about me?

In that case, next time you hear lies about you, do not let it get to you, instead ask yourself:

"Is that true? What they say about me is real?"

When that happens, you do not need to be fazed, nor fight in your self-defense. Try to remember this: history has already proven countless times, what goes around comes around, and you reap what you sow.

Take it easy, do not let anything or anyone take away your peace of mind. It is not worth it caring about others when they don't do the same to you. Simply believe in yourself, in your essence and even if you have failed and many people are pointing fingers at you, forgive yourself, change what was wrong, get back on your feet to become a better person, use this situation to grow up and try to do things differently.

Oh, understand that the same principle applies to you. Do not criticize, do not belittle anyone, do not do to others what you would not wish others did to you.

Usually, people who are always criticizing, pointing fingers or grumbling about others are petty people, poor in spirit, with no focus on their own lives, they have plenty of time to analyze other people's flaws, but not a single minute to analyze their own empty existence. Therefore, you should not be upset over such small things.

This paranoid trait of pointing fingers is not found in elevated souls...

The old saying "the tree that bears fruit will be stoned" comes in very handy. Only those who try to do something different are criticized. However, understand that what doesn't kill you will feed you, will make you stronger and whole. Every hardship brings with itself great opportunities.

Choose not to be upset by those things, do not let it affect you, instead use the stones to polish yourself, use the criticism to carve your path and skills to become even better.

If we start bothering with such petty issues, we will get smaller too, we will lose focus and we will delay our lives. Do not do that! Do not lower yourself. Do not allow yourself to get to the same level of those who criticize you. You are more than that.

The infinite light of the Eternal shines upon you, his glory and life will peacefully and safely guide you, but situations like these can steal your light and fill your heart and mind with darkness, anguish and anxiety.

This paranoid trait of pointing fingers is not found in elevated souls, which are only concerned with higher life goals and they aim to leave a remarkable contribution to history.

Do not let yourself be stained by that kind of parasitic behavior. It can destroy families, whole communities and those who act that way, will allow themselves to be taken by darkness. If not in this life, I assure, in the next. Do not get involved with people like that, and if possible, even avoid their presence..

The Essence of this Lesson

When we know who we are and where we want to be, that kind of people will not touch us, they will not even affect us. Their flammable darts cannot reach us, they will be way beneath us.

Noble souls are not affected by negative and hurtful actions of others. It is not about social class, but spiritual class. Spirituality is not religiosity. It is important to notice that some people, despite going to church a lot, have no spirituality. Their spiritual maturity is low. They will criticize everyone and may even question God's own words!

Noble souls are not contaminated by the plebs.

Anyone who feels the need to belittle others do so because they have the necessity to feel important. They have a strong urge to stand out, to be better, but instead of paying the price and improving themselves, they waste their time slandering and depreciating someone else's life, so they may feel somehow better than everyone.

By trashing others, they feel elevated to a higher ground (only in their delusion), they get to look at others from their imaginary high horse and all of that is motivated by arrogance in their hearts.

That regrettable attitude changes their perception of the world. Notice that people who are constantly criticizing and grumbling think that they are surrounded by people who cannot do anything right, thus, unsuited to their own twisted vision of perfection. That is awful, because **the slanderers are not able to truly see G-d's image on others since their own image of G-d is distorted**. Therefore, their souls are filled with bitterness, anger, and ungratefulness towards life and people around them.

The 613 commandments of the Torah could be condensed in two:

"You shall love the Lord your G-d with all your heart, with all your soul, and with all your strength and love your neighbor as yourself".

We can measure how elevated a human soul is depending on how much they are practicing this mitzvah/commandment.

Stay close to those who at least try to keep this principle. This way, you will be surrounded by people who have chosen to love instead of judging, who will welcome us when we make mistakes and who believe in our progress, by loving us even more when we most need them.

Do you realize now how inconceivable it is to be upset by criticism or depreciative comments coming from people who have no commitment to life, to the Eternal or to themselves?

I wish with all my heart you have learned the essence of this lesson.

Words are seeds

Seeds of blessing or misfortune. Words can bring darkness or light, can kill or restore life. They can help ease loneliness or can cause depression. Words may build your self-confidence or destroy your own self. They can be encouraging or dismaying. Words may advise you the right way or stray you from the path. Through words you can love, hate and even kill.

You choose! You have the power to do all of that and much more. Watch out, words are seeds, they will grow, bear fruits and you will have to sow them. Seeding is optional. Sowing is not. So allow me to share with you a tiny little secret:

Choose your seeds well because **it will not take long before you eat what you have planted**!

With words you can love, hate and even kill.

Personal analysis

Read the questions carefully, think about it and answer:

1. What kind of people do you have around you? Are they people who ramble about others or prefer to discuss ideas and projects?

____

____

____

2. Remember what you have learned in chapter two: we end up becoming like those we live with. Give it a thought and answer this: what are the goals of the people you live with? What do they want to reach? What are the principles and values driving their lives?

____

____

____

3. Are these principles and values aligned with yours? What these people have been achieving in their lives is also what you want for yourself?

____

____

____

If the answer is yes, and if these people encourage you to go beyond, that is great. But if not, rethink the impact of these relationships and try to find people who will make you grow, who will turn you into what you want to be.

Task

1. Never, under any circumstances, allow yourself to damage someone's reputation.

2. Stay away from those who take pleasure in the hateful practice of defamation (gossip).

3. Be closer to people who think big and have elevated conversations, the ones who encourage you to be an even better person.

4. Never, under any circumstances, be judgmental towards others.

5. Speak in a way that your words are an act of kindness.

6. Sow words of love, peace and justice and you will harvest a plentiful, serene life.

7. JUST TODAY: Do not grumble, do not complain, do not say bad things about others (only for the next 24 hours, of the next 30 days, of every month for the rest of your life).

.

Thoughts for meditation

"Rest satisfied with doing well and leave others to talk of you as they please".

Pythagoras (570 BC - 495 BC)

Greek pre-Socratic mathematician.

"If A is success in life, then A equals x plus y plus z. Work is x; y is play; and z is keeping your mouth shut".

Albert Einstein (1879 - 1955)

A German theoretical physicist who came up with the Theory of General Relativity. One of the many pillars of modern Physics along with quantum mechanics.

"Whoever of you loves life and desires to see many good days, keep your tongue from evil and your lips from telling lies. Turn from evil and do good; seek peace and pursue it."

Psalms 34:12-14[1]

"Those who guard their mouths and their tongues keep themselves from calamity."

Proverbs 21:23[2]

"There are six things the Lord hates, seven that are detestable to him: haughty eyes, a lying tongue, hands that shed innocent blood, a heart that devises wicked schemes, feet that are quick to rush into evil, a false witness who pours out lies and a person who stirs up conflict in the community."

Proverbs 6:16-19[3]

---

1. Bible.com. Available at: <https://www.bible.com/bible/111/PSA.34.12-14.NIV> Accessed September 2020.

2. Bíble.com. Available at <https://www.bible.com/bible/111/PRO.21.23.NIV> Accessed September 2020.

3. The Message Study Bible Conversations Repack, Capturing the Notes and Reflections of Eugene Peterson. Navpress Pub Group, 2012. Print.

Chapter 11

What does the character have to do with it?

"Try not to become a man of success, but rather try to become a man of value."

Albert Einstein (1879-1955)

A German theoretical physicist who came up with the Theory of General Relativity. One of the many pillars of modern Physics along with quantum mechanics.

11

We live in an extremely unstable world. We cannot be sure of anything anymore; **it feels like everything may collapse** at any moment and people translate this unpredictability by bringing - maybe even at an unconscious level - uncertainty, inconstancy, fragility and insecurity into their relationships and decisions.

A VUCA World

Yes, we are living in a VUCA world[1]. This word is an acronym for: Volatility, Uncertainty, Complexity and Ambiguity. The U.S Army War College introduced this concept at the end of the Cold War. Volatility is about changes occurring so fast we can barely predict what tomorrow is going to be like in certain contexts of life. What leads us to uncertainty, we are living in an unpredictable world. This way, we are faced with overly complex problems,

---

1. It's become a trendy managerial acronym: VUCA, short for volatility, uncertainty, complexity, and ambiguity, and a catchall for "Hey, it's crazy out there!" It's also misleading: VUCA conflates four distinct types of challenges that demand four distinct types of responses. That makes it difficult to know how to approach a challenging situation and easy to use VUCA as a crutch, a way to throw off the hard work of strategy and planning—after all, you can't prepare for a VUCA world, right? Crisis Management Article | HARVARD BUSINESS REVIEW. What VUCA Really Means for You. Available at < https://hbr.org/2014/01/what-vuca-really-means-for-you. Accessed December 15, 2019

which in turn lead us to ambiguity, due to how vague and unclear things become.

Perhaps we can go even deeper, we might think of this VUCA world hypothesis could result directly in the lack of men of character these days?

Wanted: Men of Character

People with a strong, righteous character are rare these days and this creates a huge impact on our society, which results in how insecure and vulnerable our world is today.

There's no escaping this, the way you act will make an impact on this world, since our behavior, the way we talk and act on different occasions will influence those around us, creating assurance or insecurity, a consequence of our own love or irresponsibility.

The world was created plentiful and righteous by the Eternal and we will either maintain or destroy these things depending on our actions. Each one of us is responsible for that.

Righteous choices have an eternal value and will affect the whole world.

We need to inspire each other to seek higher levels of righteousness. This takes effort and self-giving. These are not easy traits to exercise; however, they are a trait of outstanding people.

Righteous choices have an eternal value and will affect the whole world. So, we must teach our own children and those in school the principles and values that are fundamental to their character. A child must be taught, they will not be able to choose their principles by themselves. It would be the same thing as letting them decide if they should see the doctor or not, if they should be vaccinated, or if they wish to go to school. Children cannot decide this kind of thing, they simply must do it, considering that they are not able to make the right decisions yet. Our own character works the same way. It is formed mainly through childhood, this is why it is so important that parents teach their children what is right and what is wrong, perpetuating principles and values that are most dear, instilling in them this precious view of respecting life and others.

You know, **we need strong families. Nevertheless, they will not become stronger without men of character**!

We are in dire need of this value these days and we have been paying the price for not having it. With no sense of guidance, our children are depressed, our teenagers and young adults, in existential crisis, are living the daily pain of a meaningless life. They were all raised having their needs and wishes satisfied. Parents put their children in a bubble, depriving them of any frustration and so they end up raising individuals with no emotional immunity whatsoever. They become fragile and extremely selfish, their only concern now is their life and their well-being. **How empty and small becomes a life that revolves around itself**. That is why it is so easy to give up on this life, because its value and sanctity were never taught. They were not given the lesson on how sacred life is, and how, by this principle, you must honor and respect it.

Without proper guidance, we become slaves of our own

selfish desires. According to the magnificent Rebbe Schneerson, we have a great task of "teaching children they have an unshakeable responsibility toward G-d of living in a moral and ethical way, which will allow a better future and a better world for their own children, for generations to come".[1]

No one is here by chance and merely to satisfy their own desires. We are here, created by the infinite divine mind, to grow, to develop, to work for a better world, for peace and for justice. You may say:

"Jane, this is so utopic!"

Well, I prefer to live in a utopia, thinking I can indeed change this world than living a meaningless life centered around myself.

Be someone entirely committed to the sacred value of life.

However, I know I am not living an illusion. I know what I believe in. Yes, the world can be improved by actions. It starts from small little actions. A "good morning" and a "thank you so much" will brighten up many people's lives and make a difference to so many others. Imagine then the impact of greater actions, like helping others through their pain, actions that are capable of changing someone's life, of changing a community or even a country. This is how we give meaning to life, this is how life will hold value to each one of us.

---

1. Toward a meaningful life: the wisdom of the Rebbe. pg. 63.

A Wholesome Person

A righteous character means someone entirely committed to the sacredness of life, a person aware of the impact of their actions and their words over people and over the world.

What if I have failed?

We must dominate our impulsive and negative traits to be the best we can, to make our existence and our passage through this Earth worth it.

We carry the divine spark inside of us. If we fail and at some point in life we certainly will, we must regret and change. It is that simple. There is no point in blaming yourself, endlessly mourning your actions. The important thing is being aware of it, admitting you were wrong, repenting and changing things.

The Art of Teshuva

Teshuva is a Jewish word that means return, that is, a change that leads you back to your essence. For Teshuva to be a real thing in our lives, we must take these two steps:

1. Renounce the past we are mourning.

2. A new attitude, a significant change must be made to allow us to live the present with purpose, so we can build the future we want.

What drives Teshuva

To welcome Teshuva within us, we must have some degree of restlessness, an inner feeling of dissatisfaction and discomfort about our current situation. We must be feeling unhappy by the result of our lives and through this feeling, we will be able to understand how we truly need to make changes.

Teshuva's biggest enemy

The biggest enemy of change in our lives is when we are unable to see our failures and weaknesses. It is when we tell ourselves:

"Everything is fine! I don't need to improve."

However, according to a wise man, this is also called the "Stupidity of the Heart" because when we do not recognize our own flaws, that means our self-awareness is blocked, spiritually, morally numb and this makes us idle, stagnated, unable to evolve.

How to trigger Teshuva in our lives

1. Admit the Mistake.

Acknowledge your failures and find out what areas you need to change.

2. Confess your mistake.

Confess to G-d, a friend or your therapist. It must be someone of your highest trust, who may also be able to help you overcome this struggle, who also encourages you to go beyond and to be someone better.

3. Change.

From the moment we confess and recognize that things are not going so well, what is bothering us and dragging our lives back, we feel then motivated to move forward, with a new attitude, with a new view, we will live the change, seeking daily transformation to become our best version of ourselves.

Coming back to the Essence

No matter how far you went, today you have the chance to come back. You can start over. Return to G-d, seek to develop a righteous character, seek to improve your spirituality, to live your real humanity and you will reach harmony according to your true nature: a loving essence.

Personal analysis

After reflecting on all of this, I ask you:

1. Are you happy with the person you have become?

2. Who are you and what impact have you made here on Earth so far?

3. What have you been doing to your precious life? This is a question G-d poses you too.

Task

Answer sincerely

1. Do you want to leave everything as it is or, do you want to improve? And why?

____

____

____

2. Be brave, (I know that this reflection is not an easy deal) so take a deep look into your life now and also into your past. Where have you been failing?

____

____

____

3. In which areas of my life should I improve?

____

____

____

4. What traits should I develop in a way to live to the fullest, making my existence worth it?

____

____

____

5. Seek to develop a virtuous, responsible and altruistic behavior.

Thoughts for meditation

*"Anyhow, I've learned one thing now.
You only really get to know people
when you've had a jolly good row with
them. Then and then only can you
judge their true characters."*

Anne Frank (929 - 1945)

German Jewish teenager,
a famous victim of Holocaus.

*"Watch your thoughts, for your thoughts become words,
watch your words, for your words become actions.
Watch your actions, for your actions become habits.
Watch your habits, for your habits become character,
watch your character, for it becomes destiny."*

Frank Outlaw (1856 - 1930)

Popular Texan writer and hero.

*"If I take care of my character,
my reputation will take care of itself."*

D. L. Moody (1837 - 1899)

American Editor
and Evangelist.

*"The concern with the management
of life seems to alienate human beings
from moral reflection."*

Zygmunt Bauman (1925 - 2017)

Polish sociologist, philosopher, and professor..

Chapter 12

A CITY WITHOUT WALLS

*"Do not light a fire that you
cannot put out."*

Adi Shankara (788 CE - 820 CE)

Indian philosopher and theologian.

12

Nowadays, people are looking for countless ways to reach success, to grow in life, to reach financial independence, to live prosperously and for these purposes there are many books teaching steps, formulas and endless advice. However, I should warn you, none of these recipes will likely be effective if they do not find the right mind:

An Armored Mind

Never in our history have we seen a society with so many sick, strained, exhausted, numb, delusional, desperate and hopeless minds. **Upset and dysfunctional minds are like cities without walls**, there is no protection against enemies coming to plunder and destroy.

The Purpose of the Wall

In Ancient Times, city walls made all the difference between survival and extinction. A fortified wall, with a good structure, meant not only protection but also time and **time, my dear, is not money, is life**. From a high ground they could see people approaching and if there was a potential enemy, they would be in a privileged position because they had a comprehensive view of the situation. Being in a strategically high place would offer them many advantages over the opponent.

During the course of our lives we will experience many traumatic situations. Depending on how I deal with the pain, I will either stand up, growing and maturing from adversities, or I will let the suffering linger on, by grumbling, playing the victim, thus becoming an easy target, a city without walls and pretty soon a besieged city.

So, this book is not about all those steps you need to take in order to achieve success, nor is it about the secrets to being wealthy but instead, it is about showing you the true battle we fight day and night in our minds, in which many times we are trapped as slaves of our own thoughts.

The Battle of the Mind

Thoughts that torture and trap us will hold us back, preventing us from moving forward. In this prison, we are captives of memories that torment us, we watch ourselves become victims of this anxiety without knowing how to get rid of this nightmare.

In face of this drama that we are living daily, we feel so bound and chained that no matter how hard we try, we can hardly put into practice the wonderful recipes of those books about success and growth.

We need to be acquainted with the thieves that have been looting our minds day and night, so we can turn the tables and loot them back, taking the power off their hands. We need to effectively understand the ways of our real torturers: our own thoughts. How can our own thoughts cause this much damage in our lives? How can they boycott us, sabotage us, when we most need their help?

First, you need to understand the following concept.

You are what you eat!

"What do you mean, Jane? Weren't you talking about minds and thoughts, and now you start talking about food?"

Yes, my dear. Just as your body is a direct result of how you eat, so is your mind. Let me explain.

The Food of the Mind

You nourish your mind in several ways. There are front doors through which it is mainly fed, with our senses being responsible for this task. This way, **your thoughts are a result of everything you see, hear, talk, smell, feel and touch**. All information received by the five senses will fuel your mind, forming your thoughts and eventually they will shape who you are.

We need to be very careful about what goes into our minds, what kind of things we hear, what words we say, what or who we interact with, because all of this will change how we think and will, in the long run, forge us.

Our mind needs to be fostered, sustained by elevated thoughts, should it aim to be lifted up as well. Faced with this, we must strengthen our soul with proper food, we need to refresh and enable it, like a well-trained soldier, who is prepared, secured, armed, shielded against any type of assault or setback.

The sky is not a limit for a shielded mind

A shielded mind will have no limits, no troubles will disturb its soul. A defended mind will not bow before threats, nor will it be stopped by constant assaults coming from life. It will overcome each adversity because it is well-founded.

What is a Wall made of?

Essentially, a wall has foundations, it has cornerstones. Given this, I ask you: What are your principles and values? Have you been reading good books, have you been listening to great minds in order to build an even stronger foundation?

To shield your mind, you need to nourish it with good content, by reading the best books, by having motivational conversations, by having authentic relationships, thus allowing your senses to strengthen your mind, thanks to all this healthy and positive food. Make sure to be surrounded by words of life, words that will bring meaning and guidance to your day and to the purpose of your existence.

A Fortified Wall: A Disciplined Mind

To achieve self-control, I need to be a disciplined person, by paying attention to what I see, to what I read, taking care of how good are the things I have been giving my mind. If I take control over my thoughts, in turn, I will have control over my actions. A reckless person, who says whatever comes to their mind, who harms others with words and actions, is a result of an undisciplined, egotistical and weak mind.

You do not get to acquire an undisturbed soul overnight, it takes effort, dedication and abnegation. It takes giving up things you know at a later moment will unsettle your thoughts. Therefore, refuse to feed your mind things that are not good, things that will not enhance your mind.[1]

Redoubling your Watch

To redouble your watch over your mind, it is important that you answer the following question. Without answering it, it will be hard protecting your mind or even following any steps for success, for enhancement, for a full life and for developing the undisturbed soul.

You need to know for sure the answer to the following question:

What do you want?

---

1. I encourage you to read my book: The Nine Principles of Ataraxia, How to Reach an Undisturbed Soul.

Personal analysis

1. What is your biggest dream?

____

____

____

____

2. What are your deepest wishes, in short, what do you want for your life?

____

____

____

____

____

____

Many people reach a dead end because they simply do not know where they want to go, after all, anywhere will do. In face of the grandiosity of life, they became smaller, maybe, in all honesty, they have settled for less. Given this, if you wish to shield your mind, proceed to the next page and accomplish every single task described.

Task 1

Write on a poster what you want concisely.

You may decorate the poster and then

pin it on a place you get to see every day.

From the exact moment you know precisely what you want, you will also know in which direction you should go, which steps you should take and which steps you should also avoid. So...

Task 2

Pin the same objectives

on your mind and heart.

Emotionally Unstable People

I cannot emphasize this enough, please, be careful with hot-tempered individuals. They have behavioral and psychological problems that require professional intervention. Do not try to change them. You are not the savior of the world. I genuinely believe we should help each other, but people with emotional problems, who easily lose their temper and fight everyone around usually will play the victim and use whoever is near them. Usually, this leads to suffering for the real victim - who tried to help this person feeling and being better.

Tell me with whom you consort, and I will tell you who you are

Neuroscience demonstrates today the old saying we have seen in chapter two. Try to be with people who inspire you to be better and bigger. Do not be with people who shame you with their bad behavior. Take a closer look and choose carefully who will help to shape you the way you want to be!

An unshakeable fortress

When our minds are strengthened by good things, when they are nurtured by elevated and healthy thoughts, coupled with the fact that we know what we want and what we should fight for, certainly not many things will be able to affect us, we have become a fortress.

Seek to develop those two things in your life and you will notice how well you will live; each new day will be more satisfying and peaceful.

A Clear Mind and Soul

One of the biggest blessings in life is being a lucid person.

How sad it is when, due to any pathology, someone is not aware of who they are anymore, so many people lose their memories, their own stories.

One of the biggest blessings in life is being a lucid person.

When we are in an altered emotional state, we also easily lose our minds. In fact, we abandon our humanity and we simply respond to our lower instincts, like a lion fighting for its meal.

We were not created for that.

However, there are people out there solely living in this poor state of mind. They do not seem to understand why life makes no sense and they simply don't care about it. They don't even try to investigate where the source of the problem is.

We have been given rationality, intelligence and when we develop them, we are easily able to tackle our most primitive instincts, being able to live in a noble way, thus being a human, getting back to our essence. The human essence.

Thoughts for meditation

"The man who doesn't control his impulses is always a slave of those who seek to please them."

Gustave Le Bon (1841 - 1931)

French Polymath.

"The man who doesn't control himself becomes absurd when trying to control others."

Jewish Texts

"No man is free who cannot control himself."

Pythagoras (570 - 495 a.C.)

Ionian Greek philosopher and mathematician,
founder of Pythagoreanism.

*"Intelligence is the only means
we possess to tackle our instincts."*

Sigmund Freud (1856 - 1939)

Austrian neurologist and
Father of Psychoanalysis.

*"Mastering others is strength,
mastering yourself is true power."*

Lao Tsé (601 BC)

Ancient China writer
and philosopher.

"Wherever we turn to, we see design and purpose - the mark of our creator. Consequently, each human being has a purpose, just as any particular event in our lives."

Rebe Menachem Mendel Schnneerson (1902 - 1994)

Seventh and last Rebbe of the
Chabad-Lubavitch movement.

Chapter 13

Throw the trash away!

*"A man combs his hair every morning
— why not his heart?"*

Chinese Proverb

Along the way we accumulate many things. We keep memories, happy moments, laughter, unforgettable days, as much as sad moments, bitter memories, crying and pain.

All this together may become a heavy baggage. Good memories filled with good feelings, healthy emotions are not heavy, on the contrary, they may even carry us on. Yes, due to the simple fact that words of love and kindness we get from others will take us beyond, will push us, and will encourage us to proceed. On the other hand, bitter memories, filled with fights, arguments, troubles, words of damnation and death are like heavy stones, built out of resentment, bitterness, pain and affliction. These stones become a grueling burden, in the bags we carry in our lives. We will move slower and even breathing will be a hard thing to do. The more you accumulate sadness and bitterness, the heavier the burden becomes and the beauty of live starts fade away. Your days will be empty and meaningless. Over time, if the stones are not removed, everything will become a load!

> *Over time, if the stones are not removed, everything will become a load!*

Get to the root!

I have some bad news for you. If you want to solve this, perhaps there is no point in seeing a doctor, taking vitamins or getting a massage. By doing it, you could even find some relief but you will not solve it this way.

Good news there is a cure. Here is the catch, the issue is probably not in your body, which might be tired or failing you somehow, but it is about the bag you are carrying. Do a thorough analysis and check what you have inside it. Do not store bitterness, nor keep any resentment. Get to the root of the issue and throw away the trash!

...the issue is probably not in your body, but it is about the bag you are carrying.

A good collection

We must start a good collection of life memories, select the best moments and put them on a lovely shelf. Yes, joyfully remember the most incredible moments of your life and as you do it, be thankful for them. However, when it comes to losses, failures and disappointments avoid collecting them and, what is worse, avoid displaying them to everyone around. Stop this right now, please! Throw it all away.

Recycling now!

That is right, we live in a world each day more concerned about sustainability, we need to be aware of this and recycle as much as possible. That is, turning trash into something that can be used again, repurposing that content. Recycle the painful and sad memories from the past, see what you can learn from these traumatic events of your life and in which way you may use these situations to be a better and more mature person today.

Spring Cleaning

The same principle applies to your house. Just as our souls live in our bodies, which reflect our emotional and spiritual health, our houses shelter our bodies, reflecting our souls. That is right. Our houses reflect our inner selves.

If our minds are organized, if they have good and fluid thoughts, our houses, rooms, or closets will also be like that. If our minds are chaotic, if our thoughts are wild, messy and cluttered, probably, our houses will also be like that.

Accumulating Pain

People who have a hard time disposing, donating, or even selling things they do not use, like clothes that do not fit anymore or clothes they rarely use, probably, have a lot of accumulated pain in their lives. These are emotional problems not yet resolved, not yet forgiven, so they linger on. There is a chance it's a grieving process that was not quite completed. The pain of loss, of absence. So, they now accumulate other things to fill this void.

Freud stated that the cure comes through talking. Confession has an extraordinary power. So, confess, talk, express yourself. Grab that piece of clothing or object that somehow has brought you some memory and you do not even use anymore. Then hold it kindly, thank it for the time it served you and separate it for donation.

Be careful!

Because people who have a hard time letting go of their pains will easily become hoarders, both mentally and physically, by collecting unnecessary things.

Be organized in every aspect of your life!

Do not carry extra weight. Things you do not use, too many clothes, too many things from the past... useless stuff. Throw the trash away! Either by selling, by donating, or simply by getting rid of those things. Let them go!!!

A neat and clean house will open the way for good vibrations, for happiness and peace, for good health too. A messy, cluttered house is the perfect spot for the development of an ill mind.

Easier said than done, right? Getting our hands dirty and tidying things up may seem like a hard task to some people, but why is that?

Because it demands sacrifice. Sacrifice requires discipline and determination.

Many people do not like these words, others get the shivers just thinking of them. However, I ask you one more time, what do you want?

Do you really want to continue living in this mess or do you want to live to the fullest?

I would like to ask you to do something you may not be willing to do and at first it may seem like something fruitless, but a good spring cleaning will bring huge benefits to your life. It will be something huge. Friedrich Schiller once said that greatness demands sacrifice.[1]

Going beyond, conquering higher places, demands sacrifice. Greatness and excellence are what the Eternal wants for each one of us. Living below this line is living in constant dissatisfaction and frustration. It does not suit our perfect essence.

Dare to change! Have courage to do some cleaning in your life, in your house, in your soul! Get back to your essence! You will see this will make a difference. You will feel much lighter after removing all this weight.

---

1. Schiller, Friedrich, and Joachim Hagner. Die Verschwörung des Fiesko zu Genua : ein republikanisches Trauerspiel. Frankfurt am Main: Suhrkamp, 2010.

Personal analysis

1. What have you been carrying in your bag?

____

____

____

____

2. When you get disappointed with someone or something, do you get angry and resentful?

____

____

____

3. Do you often feel tired, even if you had a quiet day, or even after many hours of sleep? Do you feel neck or back pain or any type of muscle tension? Pay attention to those symptoms. What are they trying to tell you?

____

____

____

4. I kindly ask you to also analyze everything you have in your house, in your wardrobes and in your drawers. What is useful? What should you get rid of and what should you keep and why?

____

____

____

____

Task

1. Let your pain out.

If you have experienced a pretty difficult and traumatic moment in your life and to this day you have not properly healed, please find someone you trust, a mental health professional, a friend, or spiritual leader and let go of this trash. If you aim to live a new moment in your life, clean your soul and live to the fullest.

2. Do also a good cleaning in your house and your workplace, do not be afraid to throw away things you do not use anymore. Remember, the old must leave so the new can come up. It is your decision. Again, what do you want?

Thoughts for meditation

"Let everyone sweep in front of his own door, and the whole world will be clean."

Johann Goethe (1749 - 1832)

German writer, novelist,
and statesman.

"Don't live your life as if it were a draft. You may not have time to submit your final version."

Mario Quintana (1906 - 1994)

Brazilian poet, translator
and journalist.

"Better keep yourself clean and bright; you are the window through which you must see the world."

George Bernard Shaw (1856 - 1950)

Irish playwright, novelist, storyteller,
essayist and journalist.

*"What stronger breastplate than a heart untainted!
Thrice is he armed that hath his quarrel just, and he but
naked, though locked up in steel, whose conscience
with injustice is corrupted."*

William Shakespeare (1564 - 1616)

English poet, playwright and actor.

*"What matters the sacrifice
if the victory is honorable?"*

Helen Keller (1880 - 1968)

American writer and social activist.
She was the first deafblind person to earn
a bachelor's degree.

Chapter 14

I ABSOLUTELY LOVE MYSELF

*"A man who is always satisfied with himself
is seldom satisfied with others."*

François de La Rochefoucauld (1613 - 1680)

French writer.

14

Each one of us, as a child, was eager for life, cultivating dreams and hopes. However, each adversity we went through might have brought us to our knees, diminishing us. Gradually decreasing our self-confidence and after each difficulty, naturally, we felt more powerless and smaller than ever. Consequently, our self-esteem and self-confidence were also diminished.

In our personal journey, after hearing so many negative and destructive words, we consequently stopped believing that we deserve to be loved, that we deserve to live a better life. We may have internalized that we are not perfect and never will be, that everything is hard and that things only come with a lot of sacrifice. Then when suddenly, by a stroke of luck or fate we do find the chance to live something extraordinary and wonderful, what usually happens?

We boycott ourselves; we throw away incredible and unique opportunities. Why?

Because the hardships and uncertainties of life have striped us of the idea that we have the right to be happy.

Yes, dear, you have the right to be happy!

Understand, you deserve to be happy and to be loved.

When we start believing we do not deserve to be loved (not consciously, however our actions denounce such belief) we lose touch with ourselves, creating an abyss in the relationship with our inner self. Without a loving internal dialog, there is no way we can have a loving dialog with another person. If we are hard on ourselves, by extension we are also hard on others.

Life is easier when we are kind and easy to ourselves.

I am worthy of being loved

The way you interact with yourself is reflected in the way you interact with the world. Allow yourself to love! Thus, you will naturally allow love to happen in all aspects of your life. Life will simply blossom.

Learning to forgive yourself

Our failures are generally more fruitful than our successes. However, we take too long to understand this, and usually we end up punishing or even constantly criticizing ourselves by mistakes made in the past. But if I forgive myself for my failures, I will learn and grow from them, I will become wiser.

Foolishness would be continuing to make the same mistakes repeatedly. The only man who never fails is the one who never tries anything. If I look at myself in a loving way and understand that I am liable to mistakes, life becomes lighter and more pleasant.

When I forgive myself, I will open a door of love in my life.

Others as a mirror of myself

Anyone who has not learned to truly forgive and love themselves tends to reflect on others their own rejection, judgement, criticism and condemnation. Likewise, people who have learned how to love and to forgive themselves can also become a loving presence wherever they go.

Thus, when you love being in your own presence, you could easily be anywhere, with anyone, under any circumstance. However, if you do not appreciate your own company or if you have a hard time tolerating moments of loneliness, only because your thoughts disturb you, you could be with the most extraordinary person in the world, but even this person will not be able to fill this void you have, they will never complete you.

The relationship we have with others is a consequence of the relationship we have with ourselves.

The relationship we have with others is a consequence of the relationship we have with ourselves. There is a Jewish saying that goes like this, "he who is not good for himself, is not good for others". It is unbelievable, but these old sayings really carry deep truths.

If you do not accept yourself entirely, you will never fully accept the others. If you do not trust yourself, you will never be able to establish an authentic bond of trust with someone else too.

If you do not forgive yourself, if you hold a grudge and constantly criticize yourself, you will do the same to others.

Where does this hard time with our self-esteem and self-confidence come from?

Many times, it is deep within the roots of our childhood. In this particular moment of our stories, our identities and personalities are being built, and sometimes, during these important moments of personal growth, we hear many hard and negative words that ultimately get stuck inside ourselves in such a way that they keep resonating inside our unconscious minds as an established truth.

Words such as, "you are not good..., you are useless, you cannot do anything right, you are nothing but a nuisance..."

Negative statements like these may solidify in such a way that they become part of us, determining who we truly are and we eventually accept these sentences in an unconscious way. A cruel verdict!

Such moments that we usually experience during our childhood, or even as adults, have a detrimental effect on us, making us smaller and in the end we become so tiny, feeling powerless in face of any situation in life, we may even desire to end our own lives.

Words Build Us

In our journeys, words can highly affect us, shape us and impact us. **Words, both positive and negative, build the way we see ourselves and the world.**

However, no matter what we have experienced and heard, we must understand that we deserve to be loved. We have the right to live love. Because, unfortunately, considering how many horrible words we often hear or, given how often we fail, sooner or later, we internalize these things and tend to believe we do not deserve to be loved.

You Deserve to Be Loved!

So, in order for me to learn how to experience love and how to love myself, how to forgive my own previous failures, how to abolish all those bad words, I need to learn how to leave past things in the past and then I will truly understand that I have the right to be loved. Realize that:

You Deserve to Be Loved! More than that, you have the right to live love! Do you know why it is so important to understand this? Because love is one of the pillars of life. Love is much more than just a feeling, an emotion or an experience.

Love is our essence! Our True Nature!

The Eternal created us within love! You were created with love, to love. There lies your true vitality.

The Author of Life created you inside this bubble filled with love. With tons of affection and kindness, in a project designed by love, so this is our true nature: TO LOVE!

That is why when we feel loved or loving life or whoever it may be, we feel complete and WHOLE! We return to the center of our beings: LOVE!

So, I would like to kindly ask you to believe this truth and repeat after me:

I have the right to be loved!

I have the right to be happy!

I have the right to live love, in this life, here and now!

Understand, this is something that begins inside your own mind, you need to believe! Because **if you do not learn how to love yourself, you will never accept love**.

Love is our essence!

If you do not love yourself, this will unconsciously reflect on your relationships! Because if you do not know how to love yourself, you will not know how to love someone else and you will also not accept someone else's love towards you.

If you deem yourself as someone unsuited, who doesn't deserve unconditional love, not only will you throw away big opportunities in your life, but you will probably be trapped in a relationship in which you will have to "earn it". In a certain way, you are preventing yourself from living to the fullest, and that, my dear, is a serious thing!

So, from the moment I learn how to accept myself, love myself, with no criticism, judgement, or harsh sentences, everything changes.

Why do so many relationships fail?

Because one of them or even both have not learned how to truly love themselves and they have spent their lives constantly judging and blaming each other - it is worth noting that, most of the time, people are not aware of it; That is why they judge and criticize each other so much... In short, nothing is ever good.

Certainly, this could not possibly work like that.

Until we learn how to love ourselves, we will continue to criticize and judge. We automatically **project on others our own flaws**. So, instead of seeing their positive traits, we prefer to see the negative ones. We criticize instead of complimenting and motivating.

The misfortune of not knowing love

How sad it is the existence of a person who has not learned how to love themselves.

Why is it so poignant the idea of someone incapable of opening themselves up, to the point of being denied the right to live to the fullest and reject the essence of life?

Because the most beautiful thing there is in life is to love and to connect with people simply because they are what they are.

What is love?

The essence of love will manifest through purity, authenticity, kindness, compassion and justice.

Real love is: Being who you are and accepting others for what they are! So, instead of pointing fingers at others or even trying to change them, I myself will do the changes needed in my life, thus continuing to evolve, and as a result, I will change the world with my loving presence!

Our essence

Our vital nature is made of love. Affection is the substance that maintains the essence of life! Love is what gives meaning to our existence. WE ARE LOVE IN ESSENCE. So, tragic is the reality for those who have not learned how to love or how to fully commit to life.

Living the Carpe Diem of every moment with love is living our own essence, it is achieving our true essence because only love will make us whole!

A Loving Presence

People who have learned how to love themselves and how to forgive are a loving presence wherever they go. These are beings who bring joy, peace and lightness! They are a divine presence, a light which brightens the darkest alleys of the human soul.

Learning to be you

Herman Melville (1819 - 1891)

American writer.

Do not be afraid of being yourself. Some people seek inspiration from others and I see no problem in doing so, that is, until they start talking the same way, miming someone else's gestures, clothing style, and so on... they stop being themselves to be just a copy of someone else.

Be original, be yourself. Some will love you; others may hate you; it is impossible to please everyone, but at least, at the end of your life, you will not regret being authentic and true to yourself.

Respect what you like and what you do not like, respect your limits and at the same time, always encourage yourself to go beyond, seeking your personal evolution as much as you can. And please, I kindly ask you, **never betray your values and principles because of something or someone**.

Be faithful to yourself and to what you believe. Do not wish to pay the price for such treason. The cost is too high. It is not worth it!

*"Great things are not accomplished
by those who yield to trends and fads
and popular opinion."*

Jack Kerouac (1922 - 1969)

American writer.

Learning to love yourself

You need to treat yourself with love and care, embracing and forgiving yourself. Accept your limitations however, do not be bound by them. Try to be better every day so you can be proud of yourself and of your achievements too.

When you learn to love and take care of yourself, you will automatically love and trust others more easily and you may also be able to understand your limitations. You might even help others get through their difficulties, just as you went through yours.

We have learned how the way we see others is a mirror of how we see ourselves. So, if you believe in yourself, in your potential, even if you are not a superhero, you will also believe in others, even though they are not perfect.

Right now, you might be saying:

"That is right, I do not like myself, I do not really believe I can do something good with my life, because everything so far has been a great failure. It seems like an impossible task to look into the mirror and suddenly say that I love, accept and believe myself".

You know, I understand you perfectly and I also know of this feeling of helplessness that many times consumes us and seems to be in every single one of our cells. Nevertheless, I want to challenge you to change your life from now on, with the suggestions I will be sharing with you for it's never too late to begin!

Deep and Authentic Relationships

During our lives, we meet many people, we make countless friends and acquaintances. It is innate to human beings to connect. Connecting with others is an essential thing if we want to live to the fullest, so much so that many people treat their dogs and cats as their own adopted "children", going as far as including these "authentic relationships" in their wills, and in truth, they are.

Unfortunately, we must admit, many of the relationships we build during our lifetime are lacking true depth. Bauman, a Polish sociologist,[1] *has published extensively on how relationships have become fluid, devoid of real authenticity and true connection.*

And yet, what do we really need?

Given how easy it is to connect with others today, we may get closer to a lot more people than it was possible before. We are also a click away from totally distancing ourselves from others and unfortunately, due to this fact, we have become social media users with hundreds or even thousands of connections, therefore, if you look closely, only a few of these are authentic, with deeper roots. It is all very intense, but also very shallow. Truthfully, it is quite the opposite of what we need, and this is what our hearts and souls are craving for: pure, deep and true love.

---

1. To be more familiar with Zygmunt Bauman's work, please refer to Liquid Modernity, Liquid Love, or his other works.

The problem of Giving Yourself

This is where the core of the problem is. Deep and authentic relationships require you to give yourself. Giving yourself means surrendering. Such a hard thing to see these days! You **will hardly find someone who wishes to compromise; usually people want to be dominant**!

All of us have been through suffering to some extent and depending on what we have experienced; the memories we have stored, there may be obstacles and even walls in our minds and hearts. Eventually, we will certainly be in a relationship, however, we will not be truly open, because the fear of giving in and being frustrated again will dismiss any possibility of building a real and deep relationship.

Love triumphs over fear

Love is inherently linked with confidence, which is the opposite of fear. It creates mistrust, fights, intrigue, and separation. This feeling may have been generated by traumatic experiences from your personal story. **Fear is highly restraining and deprives us from living life to its fullest, because it prevents us from spreading this love we feel for ourselves and for others**. True love will reject any uncertainty, unrest or doubt. So, I will ask this again:

What do you want?

Maybe you have settled for less, maybe you are feeling comfortable with the way things are and you do not feel motivated to change, you do not want to pay the price of starting all over, however, deep inside you know you are far from living a real and authentic relationship.

I must confess I agree with you, living your life to the fullest takes a lot of work. However, you only have this life, right here and right now. Will you waste it like that? Will you adapt to it just to avoid getting out of your comfort zone?

If this is truly your case, remember, the opposite of courage is not fear, is pusillanimity **and if you are not brave enough to change, you will live your personal hell. Just a small detail, HERE ON EARTH**.

It is about making a decision

Being loved and to love are a matter of choice, a personal decision. Love is our nature; it is our true essence. Living this love is being a loving presence, which manifests through kindness, gentleness, goodwill, acceptance, sympathy, and above all, compassion. Being kind, truthful, honorable and fair to yourself and to others is an intrinsic part of this loving essence.

Love is pure

Young children are a clear example of what love is. They are simply who they are and live each moment to the fullest, enjoying the here and now.

Children are completely pure, they have no malice and they always believe what is said to them. They tell the truth with no intention of hurting anyone, simply because they say what is in their minds. You may lie to them and they will blindly believe you, because they see in you the purity and innocence of their own heart. **Children are the perfect example of what love is, because they carry within themselves the traits of what it truly means to give yourself, which is purity, innocence and lightness.**

We need to learn how to love, understanding that living it means being someone pure, authentic, whole, committed and kind. Love pursues what is true, fair and good according to the eternal principles and values.

This same love will guide you to make the right decisions, by taking into consideration things like honor, justice, kindness and compassion.

The best way to live

Without a doubt, the best way to live is simply being authentic and honest in every relationship, being loyal to who we are and to the things we believe, loving ourselves, being faithful to ourselves, looking after our principles and values.

Once we know who we are and are confident about it, we do not need others' approval by knowing our value; It's not necessary to say things we do not want to and we do not need to agree to something just to please others.

Being loyal to yourself, without getting shaken by what others think or say, having this peaceful certainty that all you need is being true to what you believe, true to yourself, and to your relationships. This is a priceless thing. This is the supreme love, because once you have learned to love, you will finally be ready to care for someone else and be a loving presence in the world as well.

Personal analysis

1. I invite you to analyze your own thoughts.

a) How do you see yourself?

____

____

____

____

____

____

b) How do you treat yourself?

____

____

____

____

____

____

____

____

____

____

Task

I want to encourage you, my dear, to put into practice right now the first two chapters of this book so you can truly live this chapter 14. Please, from now on, start:

1. Thinking the right way (stop boycotting yourself right now, stop thinking you do not deserve the best, or that you do not merit to be loved).

2. Finding the right people (Which people should get out of your life and what type of people do you want now to be part of it?).

____

____

____

____

3. Reading or listening to the enlightening thoughts (which you will find on my Youtube channel, in the **Meditations** playlist by the title: **Meditation to transform your life in 21 days**) for at least 21 days. You will also practice this meditation as soon as you wake up and before you go to sleep.

Enlightening thoughts

I love myself.

I absolutely love myself.

I recognize I am not a product of chance.

I was designed by the Creator of the Universe and I know my life has a higher purpose, and how invaluable it is.

This way, I completely accept myself and I promise from now on I will start to see the good things about myself instead of focusing on the negative things.

I forgive myself. I forgive myself completely.

I learn from my past mistakes and I become a wiser person. I also forgive those who have hurt me, who have hurt my soul, those who have abused me in whatever ways. I let these people go (say their names) just as any grudge and resentment I have towards them.

I ask for forgiveness to the Eternal, Creator of my life, for every flaw I am aware of or not. I accept G-d's forgiveness in my life.

The Eternal loves me unconditionally.

I open my heart for His Light to rule over me, and this way all the darkness in my soul will be gone. All my past traumas are healed, and the fears are nullified.

I look at myself with love and kindness, and I treat myself with deep respect and admiration.

I am an incredibly special person and I make a huge difference in the lives of everyone around me. People love to be with me because I do good to them, and even when I leave their presence, they still feel energized, renovated, and enlightened. This happens because the Eternal, Creator of all things and Author of life, lives inside of me and rules over me. He enlightens me and enables me to be the best version of myself every day.

I am exactly what He planned me to be:

An enlightened being.

Nothing is hard for me because I can do all things in him who strengthens me.

I am a winner above all and there is nothing I shall want.

I keep confident, I live in peace and joy with myself and with others.

I am love.

I am a unique being on Earth.

I am inspiration, motivation, happiness, peace, and light.

I am a victorious person. I am a loving essence.

Thoughts for meditation

"In the mirror everyone sees his best friend."

Yiddish Saying.

*"Never let people tell you that it is not worth
believing your dreams, or that your plans will never
work, or that you will never be someone...
but I know eventually we will learn, if you want
someone to trust, trust yourself, those who
believe will always achieve..."*

Renato Russo (1960 - 1996)

Brazilian singer and songwriter.

*"Believe in love.
Believe in magic. Believe in yourself.
Believe in your dreams.
If you don't, who will?"*

Jon Bon Jovi (1962 -)

American singer.

*"Everyone is a genius. But if you judge
a fish by its ability to climb a tree,
it will live its whole life believing
that it is stupid."*

Albert Einstein (1879 - 1955)

German theoretical physicist.

*"How can one fight against the perils of destiny
without the help of loyal and dedicated friends,
without a life partner, ready to share life's
highs and lows."*

Zygmunt Bauman (1925 - 2017)

Polish sociologist and philosopher.

Chapter 15

TAKE CARE OF WHAT YOU HAVE

"The only way to have a friend is to be one."

Adi Shankara (788 CE - 820 CE)

Indian philosopher and theologian.

15

The quality of our relationships is determined by how much care we put into them. There are exceptions. Some relationships are damaged due to multiple issues, among them, mental or personality disorders not fully diagnosed or treated. However, a relationship that receives special attention, that is well taken care of, that gets interest for its needs and dreams, with both parts sharing the responsibility of taking care of each other, provides enough foundation for deeper and loving relationships.

This way, what do we really need to build up deeper connections?

Let us start by saying what we do not need.

The Problem of Backbiting

"Don't talk unless you can improve the silence."

Jorge Luis Borges (1899 - 1986)

Argentinian writer.

If there is one thing that is totally dismissible in any kind of relationship are those words deprived of love, affection, sense, respect and comprehension. These are aggressive and abusive words that provoke emotional and psychological violence, causing irreparable damage and destroying any relationship.

How many relationships have been already destroyed due to cursed words? How many sons and daughters with open wounds for their whole lives because of tough words said by their parents or teachers? Shattered souls, hurt by words said at the wrong moment and in an improper way.

Do not say anything unless your words are there to build, to make stronger, to bless, to stimulate, to drive. Even an exhortation can be said in a wise and constructive way.

Our words are seeds, so we need to think well before we say them. You cannot take words back, and their effects may be devastating. How many therapy sessions could have been avoided, how many suicides could have been prevented, how many lives could have been saved from addiction?

Solid and uplifting words are the structure that forms our character and identity. **Words establish who we are**! We need to take care of people, watch over them and cherish them with words. Human beings have this innate need to receive attention and care.

The criticism that kills

"All our words are useless if they do not come from within. Words that do not carry the light only increase the darkness."

Madre Teresa de Calcutá

Another thing that relationships do not need are words that kill.

Yes, because words are destructive or constructive, and usually, they are indeed responsible for the deterioration or even the death of most relationships. Watch everything you say, the way you put your words together, because they will truly make all the difference in the quality and longevity of the relationships you will foster during your life.

How to create a Deep Emotional Attachment

Just as any solid building needs good planning and good execution, for a relationship to be strong and emotionally deep, you will need to work on a solid foundation. In a good relationship, we will find five basic elements that provide support for everything else.

The Five Principles of the Heart

I want to introduce to you now the Five Principles, which are responsible for creating a deep connection, which will make a relationship grow its roots and remain solid over the years:

ZAAPP. This word is an acronym formed by the following words:

1st: **Z**eal

2nd: **A**ffection

3rd: **A**ppreciation

4th: **P**rotection

5th: **P**urpose

1st Principle: Zeal

If you truly want to connect with someone and influence this person, you must dedicate yourself. To really take care of the other, you must be willing to give the attention needed to build up this relationship.

Establishing a deep attachment does not come overnight. It takes devotion, solid dedication and willingness in giving your best, especially the best of your time, which is the greatest resource we have in this life. In essence, dedicating your life to breathe life into this relationship.

Time, my dear, is your greatest resource. Time is not money. Time is life. You cannot get time back; you cannot purchase it. For instance, when death is upon you, you will not be able to say, "give me two more minutes". Maybe you would give everything you own for these two extra minutes, because then you would have understood that nothing is more important than the relationships we have. You would give everything you have to say that "I love you" you have never said, or that "forgive me", "I am sorry". So, **when you give someone your time, you are giving them the most precious thing you have: your own life**.

When we care about the evolution of a relationship, we must be careful not to be hurtful with words or actions, and at the same time we must stay alert so we may properly fulfill our significant other's needs.

We can find many examples of zeal in tiny details, and as small as they are, they still make all the difference in our daily lives.

For instance, when someone talks to you, do not let anything else steal your focus from the conversation. It should be eye-to-eye. Full attention. If the phone rings, ignore it, put it on silent, even better, do not touch your phone while you are talking to this person. Doing so, it would leave a horrible impression, giving the idea that you are not really interested. Therefore, as this person is talking, try to focus on what is being said, pay attention. Zenon, a Greek philosopher, and founder of Stoicism[1], said that nature has given us two ears and one mouth to warn us that we should listen more than talk.

Dante Alighieri, the Italian poet, warned us by saying, "Open your mind to what I shall disclose, and hold it fast within you; he who hears, but does not hold what he has heard, learns nothing."[2]

2nd Principle: Affection

When intelligence, kindness and affection
are used together, all human acts
become constructive.

Dalai Lama

Affection is the main ingredient for the growth and development of a relationship. The Department of Psychiatry at Washington University conducted an extensive research demonstrating that

---

1. Stoicism emphasized peace of mind, achieved through a life full of virtues, according to the laws of nature. To this school, philosophy is the art of living well, which is divided in three parts: logics, physics, and ethics.

2. Retrieved from MyBrainyQuotes. Available at https://mybrainyquotes.com/quote/72914/. Accessed August 2020.

children who have received affection from their mothers through care, and mostly through their presence, developed some sort of immunity against many disorders, like hyperactivity and attention deficit. What is more, these children were less likely to develop inadequate friendships and develop addictions.[1]

Affection is a nourishing thing. So much so that you may notice, when someone develops the habit of eating or drinking, thinking that this is just because of anxiety, they are wrong; actually, what we are looking for in a sugary treat or in a beverage is a hug, acceptance, affection. So, my dear, show your love in as many ways as you can. Gary Chapman has written an extraordinary book in which he describes the Five Love Languages. According to Gary, each person has at least two most prominent languages to show and receive love. He describes them as physical touching, words of affirmation, acts of desinterested service, quality time and affection.

So, try to notice which language your son, partner or someone else in your social circle has, and try to reciprocate this love with the right language. Many relationships also end because the couple was not able to interpret the way their significant other shows his or her love - in turn, they did not feel truly loved, let alone understood, and frustrations led to exhaustion and ultimately, to a breaking point. For instance: The husband grew up in a home where his dad worked a lot, this way he could provide for his family. He grew up internalizing love according to how his father expressed concern over his family,

---

1. Article: Research shows children whose parents nurture them early in life have enlarged brain regions linked to learning, memory, and response to stress. Available at <https://medicine.wustl.edu/news/love-and-the-hippocampus/> Accessed August 2020

by working hard; so, his primary love language was established as acts of desinterested service. Then, when his adult self finds the love of his life and they get married, what does he do to show his love? He works a lot. However, his wife, who may have Quality Time as primary love language, feels rejected by her husband, who comes home from work late at night every day and also on weekends, and instead of staying home with her, he works extra hours to provide comfort for his family. The wife, on the other hand, believes he doesn't appreciate staying home with her, because if he really loved her, he would not work so much.

Arguments pop up and the pain of misunderstanding is also there. Each one feels they are right, and actually they are. The root of the problem lies in the fact that, since they do not know their partner's love language, they could not admire and value their way of showing love, and this broken "dialog" led them to distancing and indifference, until it became intolerable enough to break them apart.

I close this talk on affection with what Khalil once said, "You give but little when you give of your possessions. It is when you give of yourself that you truly give. It is well to give when asked, but it is better to give unasked"[1] : you give just for having understood it".

3rd Principle: Appreciation

We need to cherish our significant others. We need to value their positive aspects and praise them, talk about them. We need to

1. https://www.goodreads.com/quotes/817768-you-give-but-little-when-you-give-of-you-r-possessions.

compliment them. Sometimes, we tend to highlight all the negative things instead of appreciating the positive ones, thus making our significant others unaware of how valuable they are for just being who they already are. Before talking about any negative thing, you should think well about how to communicate this, mentioning at least some qualities before bringing up what you need them to reflect on, the changes you want to see.

Try to admire, to appreciate how beautiful they are. I advise you to put into practice Skinner's Technique, where you could use positive reinforcement to motivate someone to behave in a certain way. This can be achieved with compliments, and sometimes, if you consider appropriate, with creative rewards or gifts.

4th Principle: Protection

Literally, it is offering a refuge. Please understand this, **a home is not a place, it is a person**. Be this person where your loved ones will find refuge and protection. This is the opposite of condemning, criticizing, pointing fingers and judging. Judging, my dear, hurts and repels.

Protecting means accepting others. Embracing them. Accepting others for who they are. Do not try to change anyone, we should encourage one another to be better, but not to change. Primarily, because any change will only happen if there is acceptance in the first place. From the moment someone truly feels loved, they will change to be a better person. Protecting also means giving proper credit, believing and encouraging. This way, try to stimulate and motivate, show that you believe in your loved ones. Keep in mind that **you should take care of what you have, so you do not need to cry for what you had.**

5th Principle: Purpose

A relationship must have a purpose, a path, an objective. This purpose may be set with plans, dreams and goals that will be pursued together, I mean, TOGETHER. It takes strategy, action, engagement and determination, which, in turn, will develop growth, intimacy and new possibilities. This is so because a plan you complete, a dream you achieve will be the fuel for new ideas, for actions to come, and these will build up a healthy and lasting relationship.

Get down to It

If you put ZAAPP into practice, you will be taking care of what you have besides ensuring the quality and longevity of your relationships. It is important to understand that we are not what **we have, but the relationships we build and the memories we leave.**

Personal analysis

1. How am I dealing with my relationships?

____

____

____

2. Do I do to others what I wish others would do to me?

____

____

____

3. Are my words constructive or destructive?

____

____

____

4. What are the main love languages I possess? In which way do I realize I am loved?

____

____

____

5. What are the main love languages of my closest family members and friends?

____

____

____

____

____

Task

Considering the previous analysis, identify which areas you need to change or maybe develop right away to give your relationships quality and longevity?

Thoughts for meditation

*"When ideas fail, words
come in very handy."*

Johann Goethe (1749 - 1832)

German writer, novelist,
and statesman.

*"Words have the lightness
and strength of the windstor."*

Victor Hugo (1802 - 1885)

French novelist, poet, playwright, essayist, artist,
statesman, and human rights activist of great
political activity in his country.

*"To fear love is to fear life, and those
who fear life are already three parts dead."*

Bertrand Russell (1872 - 1970)

One of the most influential mathematicians,
philosophers, and logicians who lived in the 20th century.

*"When you love you should not say,
"God is in my heart", but rather,
"I am in the heart of God."*

Khalil Gibran (1883 - 1931)

Lebanese essayist, liberal philosopher,
prose writer, poet, lecturer, and painter.

Chapter 16

TO EAT OR NOT TO EAT?

"Who eats well a single day won't get sick for the whole year."

Portuguese proverb

16

S o, the main question here is not "to be or not to be", but rather, "to eat or not to eat".

Obviously, my dear, the answer is: to eat. Eating is one of the best things there are in life. But of course, eating the right things, the right way. Some people do not eat, they swallow. **Turning your mealtime into a sacred ritual is an art**. It is one of the most important aspects of The Art of Living to the Fullest. Food is life and creates life. Without it, we would not survive. However, just eating is not enough, we need to understand how important this moment is, to internalize the impact it may have on us and on those we love.

The table as a tool

It is true, the table can be used as a tool. A powerful device that may potentially help build the most meaningful thing in life: Our relationships. It is nearly impossible to create everlasting ties or stable relationships without the table playing a key part in our lives.

Many times, we do not realize how important a table and meal moments with our loved ones are for building deeper connections. The moments at the table constitute a gathering of happiness, friendship and intimacy, together with understanding, forgiveness and remission. It is extremely relevant, in those occasions, not only sharing the bread, but also our experiences, listening to how everyone's day was, having an eye-to-eye interaction and even listening to what is not said. It is a vital thing to turn this moment into something blissful.

More than a lesson of manners, a lesson of life

It is at the table that we teach the first lessons of manners to our kids, that we learn about respect and about waiting for one another, about honoring the guests waiting for them to help themselves first, besides, it is the table the place where we find out how to use words like:

"Could you pass me that, please?" "Excuse me." "Thank you."

We may also teach courtesy and the almost lost art of complimenting and truly being grateful for something. **Parents are their children's role model and by using simple, yet appreciative and kind words, they become great teachers and set a powerful example**. For instance: "Honey, what a delicious dinner you have made. I have noticed you came home tired from work, but even though you have put a lot of effort into this meal, thank you…" and so on. Can you see how deep this is? Children will eventually internalize how everything requires a moment of dedication, abnegation, service, how all this must be appreciated, complimented, and acknowledged. One of the saddest things I have watched in the new generations is how children react to adults and elders.

The art of gratitude has practically been lost.

I often see children and teenagers asking for many things, getting what they want and yet, they are not thankful for them. They are generously served, but the people serving them are not acknowledged. What is implied then is that adults are not doing more than a favor, like it is their duty to serve, literally "subjecting" to a younger generation, a very special and gifted generation that thinks they are entitled to everything, any time they wish, and if that is not bad enough, they do not even have to say thank you, because the people serving them are only doing their obligation. This is very saddening, upsetting and if experienced multiple times, it is even crippling.

Ungrateful and spoiled children will usually turn this into a habit, which eventually becomes a negative trait of their character, and this happens because they were not taught manners at the table, they have not experienced it. It simply was not there for them. It is their parents' fault, who raised them like that, and truth be told, in the end no one around will put up with their behavior, and there comes a certain point where even the parents cannot handle it anymore... Then they look for professionals and say:

> *The art of gratitude has practically been lost, because I often see children and teenagers asking for things, getting what they want, and yet they are not thankful for them.*

"I do not know what went wrong, I have done everything for my kid. I gave them everything I did not have as a child, I have done everything for them and now I don't even know who they are anymore."

Rules and Boundaries

Children need order and limits to grow up emotionally and psychologically healthy and the table is the starting point to put this into practice. The table is the perfect tool to teach good manners. During a meal, people are supposed to be together, not scattered around the house. I also must emphasize, everyone should be seated, eating what is on the table, not just what they feel like eating or even suggesting the menu. Children need rules and this must be established at the earliest moment, not with tyranny but with love, happiness and resolve. They will understand this is the best for them and will learn to be happy from the opportunity of gathering with people for such precious moments, treasuring what their parents put on the table, learning how to appreciate all types of food and being grateful for them.

Temper Tantrums vs Gratitude

A tantrum is a form of ungratefulness

A child's tantrum is a form of ungratefulness because it is a failure to recognize one's efforts and authority, and how respectful they should be for it. All this ungratefulness is also a disruption of communication. Day by day, respect and communion will be lost. Soon, that authentic connection is also gone. When we teach gratitude to children, starting at the table, we are giving them the opportunity to broaden their visions. **Grateful hearts are open minds.** Open not only to new opportunities, but mainly to the ability of seeing how beautiful life is, recognizing the blessings brought by every moment. Because even hardships are opportunities for us to grow, to develop and to become someone better.

The best place since always

In ancient times, the table was already a strong symbol, where the meal had a vital role, and this is still alive today in many cultures. In Jewish tradition the table is a place that transcends the simple act of feeding, because it carries this meaning of a shrine at which the family gathers and experiences this sacred moment that radiates the very meaning of divine, where God, as a father, sits at the table with His children. Slaves had no right to be there, only legitimate sons, heirs, worthy sons.

Who does not know the story of the prodigal son, who leaves his home with his share of the inheritance, then squanders everything on celebrations and seeking pleasures? Impoverished and starving, living on the streets, and with no friend to help him, the son decides to come back home, asking his father for forgiveness, offering to work for him as one of his employees. The unreasonable son knew he was not worthy of being at the table with his father anymore. He then walks toward his former home, feeling miserable and regretful, moving slowly and heavily because the burden of guilt and shame made his body tired and destroyed. As soon as the father saw him, he started to run; at this moment nothing would stop this reunion, the seconds seemed like an eternity, he seemed so far away, but every step taken was another step closer to someone for whom he cried, waited, and dreamed of so much. His wide-open arms found his lost son, embraced him with so much longing and kindness. Then, the father kissed him; he loved his son deeply and forgave him. He returned home so much relieved, joyfully walking together with his loved one who was there now. Then, the father prepares an incredibly special dinner. The best things are served, a wonderful feast for someone once so lost and so miserable. As the father gives his son new clothes and his old place at the table, he then gives him back his dignity, by reinstating his place together with his family, restores communion, undoes any shame and embarrassement, and ultimately, he gives back his son the blessing of being able to experience the feeling of belonging somewhere, which is essential for a healthy life in all its aspects. We all need to know we belong somewhere, someone, a family, or a community.

Having no one to belong to is one of the most painful experiences a man may experience.

Having no one to belong to is one of the most painful things a man may experience.

The Table and Your Mental Health

The moment at the table is important because it emphasizes important things for the mental health of every human being:

1. **The feeling of belonging**: I am someone with people in my life, I am part of this family, of this clan.

2. **Dignity**: only worthy people can sit at the table. You do not just let anyone in, you do not invite strangers for dinner.

3. **Communion**: family meals create intimacy, unity, exchange of experiences, where fears and fantasies, dreams and failures are shared. So, we share things, experiences, we grow and develop together.

We may notice these three characteristics related to the use of the table as a tool in most cultures. In Jewish history, for instance, when Abraham received the Lord's angels, he prepared a feast for them, and through this, he created a powerful connection, and by that he got the greatest gift of his life: his son.

When Joseph, the despised and betrayed brother who later became a ruler in Egypt, saw his brothers again, he welcomed them with a feast, a signal of alliance and forgiveness.

If we mention, for instance, Jesus Christ, and ask people what they think is the best representation of his ministry, most will say "The Last Supper", the moment in which Christ established one of the most important rituals of the christian church, which has been celebrated for over two thousand years, and no matter how far in time we are from that period of history, this celebration is stronger than ever in thousands of minds and hearts. At that moment, with his disciples at the table, Jesus shared with them bread and wine, and those who were there with him forged an eternal alliance, so the act of eating and drinking transcended their bodies, the physical element. So, food and drink were the tools to a spiritual alliance and connection, also serving as food for their souls.

As you can see, there is something about a meal that goes

beyond the chemical elements our bodies need. **Food, when prepared and served in a special manner, will nourish not only your body, but also your psyche, soul and spirit.**

However, without noticing, we ignore his teaching and end up serving the "daily bread" to those we say we love in a very poor way, because we are not sharing this moment anymore, as one is eating at the table, another one is eating on the couch, watching tv, and a third one is eating in front of the computer, not even in the same room. We prepare the meal and simply give it to our children, surrendering to their appeals when they ask to eat whenever and wherever they want, we do not even have a dinner table anymore, after all, it is an "old" piece of furniture, some "modern" families do not even plan on having it in their homes. It is unfortunate these moments are wasted. There are things in life that once wasted cannot be brought back.

An Eternal Alliance

Meal moments are part of those precious hours we have in our lives. **The meal at the table is a sacred thing**. It unites us, it binds us; it connects, it encourages, it intertwines, it seeds good things around. As soon as we find out **our children are not lost out there, but rather inside our own houses**, and what is worse, at the table, then we will appreciate these unique and sacred moments we experience every day.

At the table, we can look at each other, talk about the day, about our fears, dreams, and wishes. The family that eats together will almost certainly remain together, because they establish a deeper and greater connection, since the table reflects the parents and children's roles. These are the times we get to know each other deeply, establishing intimacy. I must strongly emphasize that the table plays a key role in the construction of our character and identity.

Some parents are so worried about leaving their children money and assets, they make plans because if something unexpected happens, their children will be financially safe, they want to leave their children something real to hold on to. However, **the best plan we can make in life for our children is prioritizing our time and dedicating special care to them every day**. An example of this is when we prepare a meal, serving it with kindness and grace, gathering everyone around, having a unique and special moment every day, it is not a trivial thing, after all, spending time together at the table is the biggest investment we can make, it is one of the biggest legacies we can leave, because it shows how much of a priority my home is, it shows that the most important thing to me is sharing a delicious meal with those I love, enjoying every minute of this precious moment that I know will not come back.

In view of this, I believe you have captured the message. Sharing a meal with those you love is much more than just appeasing your hunger and feeding your body. A gathering at the table with your family means sharing feelings, listening, and being listened to, communicating, expressing, showing yourself, exposing yourself without fear, not just sharing the food there, but also feelings and thoughts.

Oh, but the moment at the table is a time neither for lectures nor arguments. It is when we cultivate peace, when we solidify alliances and relationships, when each family member is reassured for their individual importance. Children, and even babies on their highchairs, will feel like a part of it, accepted within the "clan". This special moment many may deem as a simple part of their routine will help our children form their character, how they should proceed, which values they should nurture, what concepts and principles they should stand by.

Happy but not perfect

It is important to remember that a happy life does not mean a perfect life, with no struggles or setbacks. If we ponder about our existence and assess our memories, we will see that our most happy moments were around the table, when we celebrated and established special moments of our paths. Therefore, it is up to us, parents, to cultivate in our homes these meals at the table, not in a formal way, but rather organized and fun, full of love, freedom, respect, and responsibility. These will be a part of our children's memories and the memories of those we love the most. These moments will be a part of this big and true legacy we can leave them with.

It is important to perceive that the quality time invested in your family meals will not only help developing and deepening the relationships between family members, but also building our children's character and identity.

Personal analysis

1. How special is the place the table has in my life and in my family's life?

____

____

____

____

2. Are meals appreciated and made exactly like they were supposed to or are they just another part of your routine?

____

____

____

____

3. Now, take a closer look at your happiest and most meaningful moments in life. Were they not at the table with special people?

____

____

____

____

Task

1. Turn your mealtime into a sacred ritual.

2. Decide to do your best when preparing meals together with those you love, also set the development of a loving dialog as a priority that will encourage the deepening of your relationships.

3. When preparing a meal (either on weekends or on holidays), invite your children to help you. You can teach them to prepare something special, or tell them how this particular recipe came to be (even more interesting if it's a family recipe, with the details on how grandma or anyone else would have it prepared), so you may have fun moments together, showing how delicious and interesting and delicious cooking can be, by savoring the pleasure of this moment. Children love making crackers, creating shapes, kneading bread, rolling out the dough to bake it. When they finally see the result of what they have made themselves, it is hard to describe their happiness and satisfaction. It is worth living such deep meaningful moments..

Thoughts for meditation

*"When I was a kid, I had to be quiet at the table:
only the adults did the talking. Now, after I am an adult,
I have to zip my mouth for the kids to talk."*

Mario Quintana (1906 - 1994)

Brazilian poet, translator, and journalist.

*"Better is a dry morsel with quiet than
a house full of feasting with strif."*

(Proverbs 17:1)

*"A good upbringing means not that you
won't spill sauce on the tablecloth, but that
you won't notice it when someone else does."*

Anton Tchekhov (1860 - 1904)

Russian physician, playwright, and writer, considered
one of the greatest writers of short fiction of all time.

*"All great change in America
begins at the dinner table."*

Ronald Reagan (1911 - 2004)

American actor and politician, the 40th president
of the United States and the 33rd governor of California.

*"Simple meals, water to drink, bent
elbow for pillow: there in is happiness."*

Confucius (551 - 479 A.C.)

Chinese philosopher and thinker.

Chapter 17

GIVING IS BETTER THAN RECEIVING!

"Someone is sitting in the shade today because someone planted a tree a long time ago."

Warren Buffet (1930 - Present)

American investor.

17

Great psychiatrists, well-known scientists and professionals of several areas of knowledge have been thoroughly searching and studying about the meaning of life. The answers they have found, in the end, converge to just one. Life finds its purpose in the connection with others, with community integration, with the role humanity itself plays, in how much my existence and attitude will make a difference by making other people's lives worth it.

Viktor Frankl, Austrian psychiatrist, went through the horrors of Holocaust, lost his whole family and his pregnant wife to the Nazi concentration camps. While experiencing this savagery, he noticed that among the survivors, there was something in common: a higher sense of purpose in life. The most incredible thing is, their purpose was not related to themselves, to their dreams and to their personal goals, however taking care of others instead. They found the value of their own lives by serving others, by doing something in this world to make it better than it was before.

> *They found the value of their own lives by serving others, by doing something in this world to make it better than it was before.*

The First and Foremost Teaching

If I want to lovingly give with no attachments, I must first learn something important in my life. I must learn the great lesson of receiving. That is right, my dear!

People who donate big sums, who give their best to this life, who contribute with the dearest treasure they have here, their own time, are people who know they themselves are extremely rich and prosperous in the first place. You cannot give something you do not have.

Some people are financially wealthy, but they are not satisfied with what they already have, so they live in this continuous frenzy, this eternal search for more, because they have this feeling they lack something, that something is not right and despite their fat bank accounts, they do not see themselves as prosperous because scarcity is unconsciously deep within their own minds.

You cannot give something you do not have.

The stream that flows

The notable teaching that we will learn here is that to offer something, to be someone who lovingly gives, it does not matter what you already have, but what you know is already coming your way. If, for instance, I see life, the Eternal's love and all His blessings flowing through me, by bringing opportunities to me, bringing special people, I can see (through the eyes of faith) providence blessing me like a waterfall, like a constant stream, so I will give some of what I have and of I what I am, with no fears, no demands, without being concerned about it.

I will happily give, because I understand that as I bless someone, I will be blessed. As I share, I will multiply what I have. As I give, I will have even more, because less is more by this account, I understand and I simply know that this stream is permanent and it will flow endlessly.

The Secret

There is a secret here. Those who get to learn it during their lifetime are quite rare, however, once they acknowledge it, they start living their lives in abundance.

This great and priceless secret, my dear, is **giving with joy**. It is the act of giving without the feeling of losing. From the moment I give with joy, an endless chain of good things and feelings will come and it is something really incredible, because as I give, I will also receive, the doors will open in multiple ways and the Shalom prosperity will simply flow. The universal law of sowing and reaping applies here.

However, giving with joy involves another secret, a deeper one. To learn how to give with joy, with your heart truly open and unselfish, you must first learn another lesson.

The Art of RECEIVING

It may sound odd but receiving also requires some skill. Until this moment, how much have you learned about being receptive to things? Or every time someone gives you something or blesses you in some way, you simply say: Thank you, but there was no need...or you will just refuse it and promptly say:

"I am sorry, but I cannot accept this" (because in your unconscious mind you think, "I did not do anything to deserve this, I must earn something through much suffering, struggling, and sacrifice, so, I have no right, I do not deserve it").

The internalization of these concepts has made you cease the flow of gifts life has for you, because you either think you have not earned it, or you must do more in order to rightfully accept it; or maybe it is just not the moment yet, as if you could judge such a thing.

It is free!

You know when you are buying something you need and there is promotion going on? Something is being offered in a special, beautiful package, two of them you already need, and there is another one that comes for free. What do you do, do you buy this product with the usual price, or do you get the box with the best price plus an extra?

People will usually take advantage of such opportunities, feeling fortunate as they are getting something without paying full price, and they do not even think twice, accepting the offer right away (who would refuse it?).

Once you start realizing you are more blessed than you think, and how these small things you get every day are real blessings, then you will become aware of how wealthy and plentiful you are. Life will, thus, simply flow even more than before.

When you start your day, no one will be telling you something like "look, today you will have to breathe less because the air is limited"... or imagine on a cold day, as the sun is coming out, all you wish is for free sunlight to warm you. No one will tell you, "Well, the sun is out, but you will only get three minutes to warm, I shall ask you to leave after this time." No! Nature is plentiful, it gives beyond measure!

When we are aware and grateful for the many blessings around us, in the form of authentic connections and relationships, good health, work, or nature itself and when we realize the Grace in all of this, life simply turns into this delightful Give-and-You-Shall-Receive adventure.

Charis

In the ancient Greek world, it was customary for people to greet by saying: "Charis" (which meant I greet you with a favor).[1] Paul, the apostle, in order to unite the Greek and the Hebrew world, started greeting people with: "Grace and Peace". Why? Because just as the Greeks used Charis for saying hello and goodbye, the Jews used Shalom.[2] So, to include everyone in their initial greeting, Saint Paul started his letters by saying:

---

1. Read more about it in: Sparkling gems from the Greek Vol 1. Rick Renner.

2. Read more about Shalom in my book The Nine Principles of Ataraxia. The nine principle

Grace and Peace! Charis & Shalom!

Which meant "I salute you with grace (favor) and peace".

It is so beautiful!

You should learn to receive favors from the world, from the Eternal, from people, from life!

Learn to receive favors from the world...

Open your arms to receive and to give. Look at how beautiful life is, how plentiful and how constantly prosperity flows in all its aspects. It is about recognizing, saying thanks, receiving, loving and in turn, giving as well.

Humility

I do not think it is possible to be a true giver without humility. I need to be confident that I rely on this constant flow, I need to surrender to it, and **for that I need to be detached from myself, from my arrogant desire of having everything** in my hands, of being in control of everything. So, to be someone who truly gives, I must humbly learn to put myself in the position of also being a receiver and then the blessings will flow like a river. This way, I must act as a mere conduit that will also pour blessings into other people's lives. In this fashion, the more I open my arms with the intent of giving, the stronger this flow of blessings and prosperity will be in my life.

---

of Ataraxia is Shalom. By reading it, you will know more about this conceptual treasure.

Learning how to give is so much better after you have learned how to receive, my dear. So, open yourself to the blessings destined to you in this life, spread your arms from now on and say:

I am ready

I am open to receive all the blessings destined to me since before the creation of the universe.

I am open to freely receive it and i allow myself to be a recipient to the flow of the eternal in this life for all sorts of blessings and prosperity.

I am completely and definitely open to give and receive.

Personal analysis

1. From 01 to 07, how much have you been willing to give until now? Why?

____

____

2. What thoughts usually come to your mind, preventing you from sharing either what you have or what you are?

____

____

3. From 01 to 07, how much have you been open to receive?

____

____

4. What thoughts usually come to your mind, preventing you from freely receiving what life offers you?

____

____

____

5. Where do you think these limiting thoughts come from? Look for the roots of these arguments. Do not discard the first thoughts that came to your mind, write each one of them below.

____

____

____

Task

1. Write a gratitude journal, by taking daily notes of at least three good things that you have experienced during your day. This simple activity will make you aware of all the abundance flowing in your life through different ways. Maybe you have not noticed so far how intense it is (write to me about the result of this task later, practice it for at least seven days in a row).

I am grateful for...

1st Day

1.____

2.____

3.____

2nd Day

1.____

2.____

3.____

3rd Day

1.____

2.____

3.____

4th Day

1.____

2.____

3.____

5th Day

1.____

2.____

3.____

6th Day

1.____

2.____

3.____

7th Day

1.____

2.____

3.____

Thoughts for meditation

"Friendship and cooperation are not merely sentimentalistic or idealistic wishes, but also real means to make us stronger."

Indira Gandhi (1917 - 1984)

Former Indian prime minister.

"Love is an activity, not a passive affect. it is a "standing in," not a "falling for"... love is primarily giving, not receiving."

Erich Fromm (1900 - 1980)

German psychoanalyst, philosopher and sociologist.

*"As our very lives begin and end with
a need for affection, would it not be better
to practice compassion and love towards
others when we are strong and capable?"*

Dalai Lama (1937 - Present)

Head of State and
Tibetan spiritual leader.

*"The spirit grows with what it receives,
the heart with what it gives."*

Adi Shankara (788 CE - 820 CE)

Indian philosopher and theologian.

*"What I do is simple: I put bread
on the tables and share it."*

Madre Teresa (1910 - 1997)

She was an Indian-Albanian catholic,
founder of the Missionaries of Charity, whose
charisma was at the service of the poor.

Chapter 18

SURPRISE!

"Those who can't contemplate (the world) with astonishment, have their eyes closed."

Albert Einstein (1879 - 1955)

A German theoretical physicist who came up with the Theory of General Relativity, one of the many pillars of modern Physics along with quantum mechanics.

18

We are humans. And, as such, we can easily get too comfortable. We are hard workers, we cross our limits, we do everything to reach our goal, whether it is a car, a new job, or a higher job position. However, as soon as we accomplish what we want, we tend to relax, we sit on our hands.

We are masters in the art of impressing, of overcoming, of surprising, but after we have achieved the prize we craved so much, we usually settle for it, even worse, we get so comfortable we even stop treasuring what we have achieved, which could lead us to lose this object, this asset or even this person.

When we develop the art of constantly astonishing, we avoid this kind of risk. Have you ever been taken by surprise when you got home after an exhausting day, and as you get inside your house, tired and hungry, taking small steps because you lost all your strength, suddenly you realize this delicious smell in the air of cozy food just waiting for you.

You cannot believe your eyes as you see a full table and your partner waiting for you with a glass of wine?! This is worth more than gold. This is what builds lasting relationships. **Surprising! Doing a little more than expected!**

Dare to change the old

To surprise someone, you need to be brave enough to innovate, to do something different from the old ways. You need to be bold. For this, you need to be daring, you need to push yourself harder, you need to think outside the box.

I admit this takes effort and planning.

The same old thing, my dear, is tiring and depressing. It is also tedious and ordinary.

Surprising is like flying. You need to spread your wings for it to happen. This takes attitude and detachment. Attitude because if you want to surprise you must act. Detachment because if you want to fly, you cannot be carrying lots of things, your arms must be free. You need to be free to truly live this. To give yourself. It is that simple! However, it does not mean simple is easy. You know why?

Because in order to amaze, you must let go of everything you already know, of everything you have already done, you must reject the same old ways and switch from what is certain to what is uncertain.

Doing something different is giving up your comfort zone, getting out of this place you feel safe and simply having the courage to risk failure.

Surprising is like flying. You need to spread your wings for it to happen.

Boost your creativity!

Surprising is putting your creative power into motion. It involves action and a good dose of enthusiasm. I agree that doing so requires a lot of effort, because we need to face the fearful bogeyman of insecurity, but only through the motivation of these challenges will we be able to grow and mature.

Impressing does not always mean doing hard things. You may also bring surprise with something simple. However, truthfully, sometimes keeping things simple is a complex thing to achieve. But you should dare to believe and accomplish it!

You do not want to live the tragedy of an existence based on usual things. Let yourself experience the adventure of living to the fullest and seek to surprise every day, especially yourself. It is a delightful thing to do and I believe it is a wonderful feeling when you look at yourself and say: "Wow, I have done that!"

The feeling of accomplishment fills you with this healthy pride, which is also good for your self-esteem and self-confidence. So, my dear, allow yourself to surprise and amaze!

People who surprise with their existence

Amazing people are extraordinary and there is a good reason for that. They are not attached to material things; they are attached to people. An extraordinary person lives each moment by giving themselves fully. They give themselves and open up before leaving, they donate before they die.

People like this are irreplaceable, they are extraordinary and unique, singular in all aspects. They also make you feel unique and special when you are with them. They listen to you carefully. They watch you in tiny details and compliment you, even when you do the slightest thing. They may even obtain many material possessions during their lives, but after they are gone, those things are not valuable anymore, losing their importance. Why? Because the importance was on their unique and extraordinary loving presence.

What lesson have we learned then?

Being surprising is making your life prettier, your days lighter and more delightful, guided by affection, creativity and dedication; a loving dedication to who you are and what you do.

Daring is not just wildly doing something. It is being someone impressive. It is delivering my best version of myself today. It is doing my part in mankind's history. It is building a legacy. Yes, I know, all this takes effort. But it is worth it! Because nothing, my dear, is worth the emptiness of a lazy life. It is also about being responsible, understanding that, if I do my best, I am contributing with a drop of water to this huge ocean life is.

...nothing, my dear, is worth the emptiness of a lazy life.

Personal analysis

1. In which areas of my life am I too comfortable and now that I have noticed, should I stir things up and surprise?

____
____
____

2. What ideas and actions should I put into practice to impress in all areas of my life?

Personal:____
____
____

Family:____
____
____

Partner:____
____
____

Friends:____
____
____

Spiritual:____
____

Other aspects of Life:_____________________________
____

Task

From now on, set as an objective to surprise yourself by seeking to be a better person each day, wherever you are.

Amaze by giving your best, by being the best version of yourself right here and right now!

Thoughts for meditation

*"Our lives are defined by moments.
Especially those who take us by surprise."*

Bob Marley (1945 - 1981)

He was a Jamaican singer, songwriter, and guitar player,
the most famous reggae musician of all time,
known for popularizing the genre.

*"Everything that is new or uncommon raises
a pleasure in the imagination, because it fills
the soul with an agreeable surprise, gratifies
its curiosity, and gives it an idea of which
it was not before possessed."*

Joseph Addison (1672 - 1719)

English poet and essayis.

*"When we are no longer able to change
a situation, we are challenged
to change ourselves."*

Viktor Frankl (1905 - 1997)

Austrian neuropsychiatrist and
psychoanalyst, founder of logotherapy.

*"Baudelaire said that surprise and astonishment
are basic characteristics of an artwork. I feel the same way.
Camus, in The Stranger, says that reason is the enemy
of imagination. Sometimes you must put reason
aside and make something beautiful."*

Oscar Ribeiro de Almeida Niemeyer Soares Filho (1907 - 2012)

He was a Brazilian architect, considered a key
figure in the development of modern architecture.

Chapter 19

CARPE DIEM

"He who puts off nothing till tomorrow has done a great deal."

Baltasar Gracián y Morales (1601 - 1658)

Spanish Jesuit and writer from
the Spanish Golden Age.

19

We only get to live a small fraction of our lives. Do a quick math. How much time of your existence has been wasted with:

- Unnecessary suffering;

- Anxiety and worries;

- Petty satisfactions;

- Worthless conversations;

- Futile passions;

Time is passing RIGHT NOW, exactly at this moment it is slipping away.

Time has a small and important feature:

It does not come back.

Everything we see or touch dissolves.

I will do it tomorrow!

Procrastinating is the worst addiction; it steals the present by promising a future that will most likely never be here.

Some people are anxious about their future and yet they are living a boring life in the present, without ever fully enjoying the real 'Carpe Diem'.

Carpe Diem?

This Latin aphorism, which literally means "pluck the day", was first used by the roman poet Horace, in a stoic-Epicurean inspiration, while he was writing to Leuconoe, in his first Odes book, still in 23 BC, advising her to enjoy the best of life at each moment.

Unfortunately, some people will take this literally, falling into hedonism, by living a reckless and irresponsible life. However, the great lesson lies in living our days as wisely as we can, developing our full potential today, seeking to live an extraordinary life, giving my best contribution to Earth, right here and right now.

Diving without Fear

Do not be afraid of diving into the present, of getting rid of ties with the past and anxieties about the future. Simply dare to give yourself, dare to truly live.

Now is all we have. Many times, we throw our existences into a pile of bitterness, sadness, and past failures.

We dilute our present in this wicked anxiety about the future that awaits us. In both cases, we are missing the great opportunity of living the present to the fullest.

But how should we live each day to the fullest?

It is simple - by establishing priorities. Let me illustrate this with a brief story.

A philosophy teacher brought with him a big glass jar to use during his class. He also had a box full of stones. He put the stones inside the jar, one by one, until the jar was full. Then, he asked the students.

"Is the jar full?"

"Yes. It's full", they answered.

Then the teacher took another box filled with marbles. He poured them inside the jar, and as he gave it a shake, the marbles started moving into the empty spaces between the stones. Once again, the wise teacher asked:

"Is the jar full?"

"Yes", they replied, "now it is completely full".

Much to their surprise, the teacher picks up another box and starts to slowly pour sand over the rocks and marbles already there. The sand gradually filled up all the remaining empty spaces. Again, the teacher asked the students:

"What now, is the jar full?"

The students, now intrigued, trying to understand what message the teacher was trying to give them, firmly agreed:

"Yes, dear teacher. Now the jar is completely full."

Then the teacher started explaining:

"This jar, my dear students, represents life. The stones are our priorities. Things that really matter, like your family, your partner, your children. The stones are the priceless things in life and even if, at some point, you lose everything else, the stones will be there, your life will still be whole.

The marbles are other important things, like your job, your house, things you own.

The sand is the rest of the things in your life, the little things, like distractions and even our worries.

If you pour the sand into the jar first, then there will be no space for marbles or stones. The same goes for life." If you spend your time and energy on small things, things that do not matter, there will never be space in your life for the things that really matter. So, pay attention to what is truly meaningful to your happiness. **Set your priorities and avoid pouring sand instead of stones**.

Stay close to who you love, develop authentic and deep relationships - this takes time, creativity, prioritizing things. Love, forgive, give yourself, and do not neglect the things you care about, do not postpone what truly matters to you.

A whole life in a single day!

Live each day as if it were your whole life. Do not expect tomorrow - you may not have it. You cannot change what is gone, so why dwelling in the past, blaming and constantly criticizing yourself or even others?

Give yourself entirely to the moment and live today as though there is no tomorrow.

Give yourself entirely to the moment and live today as though there is no tomorrow.

Here is what you should do: try to live one day, just one day like this, by giving yourself completely, entirely living the present and you will see how much of a difference it will make! Tell me later about it, ok?

Because we usually say:

"I will do it tomorrow!"

"I will say it tomorrow!"

"I will apologize tomorrow..."

"I will say I love you later..."

The Unforgiving Minute

Dear, tomorrow may not even come, there might not be enough time left, so truly, tomorrow may be too late.

Living life well is, indeed, knowing how to manage your biggest and most precious asset: time.

Living Carpe Diem does not mean you should live wildly, not at all, you should live in an intense and balanced way. And what is the reward of choosing to live and not just to exist?

Quite simple, living now will bring you peace in the end! Knowing how to live, how to enjoy every moment, by not leaving things behind, like words, gestures, or loving actions, will ensure your peace of mind when that time comes: passing away.

Now, maybe you are saying:

"Jane, for the love of G-d, this is shocking!!!"

My dear, we are on a long road, to grow, to develop, and then we will leave.

Death is a taboo in most conversations, but it is the most certain thing in life. Life and death are intrinsically interconnected. And you will only live your life when you are aware of how certain and unavoidable death is.

Do not live as if you were eternal, you are dust, and to dust you will return. "You are food for worms", as Professor John Keating rightly said, warning his students to live Carpe Diem.[1]

"You are food for worms"

Live in a dignifying way, by experiencing every present moment, by giving meaning to each second, by making your existence count, and as brief as it may be, it can still be immensely meaningful.

---

1. Check this out in the film Dead Poets Society.

It all depends entirely on YOU! Remember, **you are not what you have, you are the mark you leave behind. So, choose the memories you want printed in the mind of the people who lived with you**. Leave the mark you want now, set your priorities today, love and give yourself, living each second of this gift that is HERE and NOW.

Personal analysis

Do a thorough analysis of yourself. Where do you (truly) live?

a) In the past - I confess I cultivate many of the sad moments I have experienced, I hold many grudges against people who betrayed me, against hard words I have heard...

b) In the present - I live the HERE AND the NOW, completely enjoying the present. My life is a constant CARPE DIEM!

c) In the future - I am always anxious about what is going to happen, what I could prevent from happening...

2. Given your answer, and considering you did not choose letter B, what will you do from now on to seize the day? Write it down because words are powerful tools to determine your next steps.

____

____

____

____

____

____

____

____

____

____

____

3. What are your priorities in life, the things that truly matter to you?

____

____

____

____

4. How much time do you spend on them?

____

____

____

____

Task

1. Never wish to find out on the verge of death that you simply did not live properly.

Choose to live in an intense and balanced way, boldly diving into this adventure that LIFE is!

2. Throw away any fears and dare to do it!

3. Live the Here and the Now!!!

Thoughts for meditation

"No project is viable if you do not start working on it right now: the future will only be what we have started making of it today."

Içami Tiba (1941 - 2015)

Brazilian psychiatrist and writer.

"You need to love people like there is no tomorrow, because if you think about it, there really is no tomorrow."

Renato Russo (1960 - 1996)

Brazilian singer and songwriter.

"When I was young, I told my dad,
"One day, we will be rich and we will have a
big house", then he told me, "Son, this is impossible".
Well, today I have everything I told my dad
I would have, but I don't have my dad anymore."

Cristiano Ronaldo (1985 - Present)

Portuguese footballer, he is considered
one of the best players of all time.

"He who knows most,
grieves most for wasted time."

Dante Alighieri (1265 - 1321)

He is considered the first
and greatest Italian poet.

"Let us go to our sleep with joy and gladness;
let us say, "I have lived; the course which
Fortune set for me is finished."
And if God is pleased to add another day,
we should welcome it with glad hearts."

Lucius Annaeus Seneca, letter 12,9 (4 BC. – AD 65)

He was one of the most prestigious lawyers,
writers and scholars of the Roman Empire.

*"Real generosity towards the future
lies in giving all to the present."*

Albert Camus (1913 - 1960)

He was a French-Algerian writer, philosopher,
novelist, playwright, journalist and essayist.

Chapter 20

BETTER LATE THAN NEVER

"Vitality shows in not only the ability to persist but the ability to start over."

F. Scott Fitzgerald (1896 - 1940)

American poet, writer, novelist, storyteller, and scriptwriter.

20

You might be thinking: "There are so many things I have learned from this book so far, but also many things went wrong in my life; I think now it is definitely too late. If only I could start all over, but this knowledge came too late to me..."

What I mean to tell you is:

Better late than never, my dear!

It is never too late to be who you really want to be. To fight to get the life you want, to accomplish your dreams, to live what you have deemed impossible so far. Now, with all the knowledge and practical wisdom these chapters have brought, you are able to completely transform your life, starting a new journey filled with passion and determination.

It is never too late to be who you really want to be.

Life is Sacred

Be aware that **it is never too late to learn how sacred life is, how we should enjoy it the best way we can**, by fulfilling our mission on this Earth, by loving and doing our part so the world may also be a Home Sweet Home, a more welcoming and loving place for as many people as possible. It is never too late to begin. If you have lived many frustrations and disappointments, do not despair, it is not too late to start over too, to dream and to make things happen.

I made a sample list of interesting things to do before we die. I will start by giving you some examples asking you to fill out this list with what you wish to do, and remember this again: better late than never.

List of Things to Do Before you Pass Away

1. Be closer to those who really matter;

2. Read an epic book from start to end;

3. Watch the Aurora Borealis;

4. Write a book;

5. Make the trip of my dreams with_________________________;

6. Visit an old friend;

7. Anonymously help people in need;

8. Live a great love story;

9. Learn a new language just to visit a country, to talk to the locals and to learn their culture.

10. _______________________________________

11. _______________________________________

Personal analysis

Reflect on how you have been living your life:

1. Am I making the most out of my time?

____

____

____

____

2. Have I been making a sacred home out of this world? A better place to live?

____

____

____

____

3. How much effort have I put into making my dreams come true, considering how it is better late than ever?

____

____

____

____

Task

1. **Make a kind gesture as a way of showing gratitude for your existence**. Such an attitude warms the Eternal's heart, because He will see that you, whom He believed and invested his best in, is seeking to develop your potential. So, you will see, His love blessings will again be multiplied and sent to you.

2. Now, put into practice the list you have completed above. Set a schedule to do these activities and put them on your calendar. This will keep them in your memory and will encourage you to truly live what you want to live before you die.

3. In the next page, I have written some thoughts for affirmation and meditation during 21 days. Remember what we have learned in the First Chapter: we are what we think; so, you need to be surrounded by the right thoughts if you really want to achieve all the plans and dreams you have for your brief existence on this Earth.

Thoughts for affirmation and meditation

"I am G-d's beloved child.
My life has a purpose.
Neither my birth was an accident,
nor am I here by chance.
My life matters.

I am a key part in mankind's history.
I am an irreplaceable person. I am priceless.
This way, every second is precious and filled with
meaning. G-d has chosen for me to live here.
He invested his will, his creativity and his energy
in my creation. My life lies in who
I AM and He is guiding me so I may live in harmony
with the purpose of my existence on Earth.

In face of this, I decide to live to the
fullestandin a serene manner.
Because everything has a given purpose.
I learn from everything and everyone.
I make of this place a better place to live
by the simple fact of existing, along with
my commitment to do my best
every day of my life."

Thoughts for meditation

"Let no one ever come to you without leaving better and happier."

Mother Teresa of Calcutta (1910 - 1997)

Albanian-Indian catholic nun, known as the
Saint of the Gutters and Nobel Peace Prize winner in 1979.

"I sometimes hear the wind blowing through and it feels that for the sake of this bliss, being born was worth it."

Fernando Pessoa (1988 - 1935)

Portuguese poet, philosopher, playwright, essayist,
translator, advertiser, astrologist, inventor, businessman,
literary critic and political commentator.

"From my telescope, I saw God walking!
The marvel, the harmony and the organization
of the Universe could only be achieved in accordance
with a plan from an almighty, omniscient being."

Isaac Newton (1643 - 1727)

English astronomer, alchemist, natural philosopher,
theologian, and scientist, more widely known as
physicist and mathematician. The three Newton's
laws are fundamental to classical mechanic.

Chapter 21

WHAT MEMORIES WILL YOU LEAVE BEHIND?

*"The best preparation for tomorrow
is doing your best today."*

H. Jackson Brown (1940 - Present)

American writer.

21

L ife is a gift. A daily gift from the Eternal. However, **life is not eternal**. At least not here. Lifehere on Earth has a beginning and an end. The big mystery lies in the fact that we do not know what day it will end, nor how it will end.

Life is a gift.

In this book, I talk about many ways or actions we must develop so we can live life and enjoy life to the fullest. However, **there is no way to talk about life without talking about death**.

Martin Luther King Jr. once said that a man is only ready to live when he is finally ready to die. However, what truly makes us ready for this moment?

When are we ready to die?

We could speculate about it, but I will only talk of my own convictions. A person is only ready to say goodbye to this life, dying in peace, when they are sure they have fulfilled their purpose here on Earth. Yes, someone is only ready to leave this life, to say goodbye to their loved ones and to go with a light soul when they are certain they have completed their work here.

Maybe you are saying now, "Jane, now things are really confusing... but anyway, how do I find my purpose, or how do I know I am truly fulfilling it?"

Our purpose is intricately linked to the meaning of our lives. I am not talking about major accomplishments, like acquiring material things, or even professional and intellectual growth, but just about BEING.

Someone's purpose is deeply associated with what they are and this covers all aspects of their lives. For instance, imagine a nurse - let's call him Mark - who, while doing his job, not only tends to the sick and helps the doctors, but also relieves the people's pain with his smile, consoling them with his words, bringing wellness wherever he goes. Mark is someone who not only fulfills his social role as a citizen and a professional, but he goes beyond, he makes the lives of those around him better in many ways. He does it by just BEING someone who, either in his home, out there, or in his work, is always performing his role with primacy, sharing his life with others, helping others find hope while in pain and as he brings wellness to them, his own life finds meaning.

When we help other people with their struggles and difficulties, contributing to the development of a broad and improved life view, not only the existence of those we help becomes more meaningful, but ours too. Thus, **if we help others find meaning in their lives, our own lives will find meaning**. This is how it works. It is quite simple.

What if life no longer makes sense?

People who are only concerned about their own interests, seeking nothing but accumulating assets and money for their own pleasure, will experience, at some point during their poor lives, deep existential crises, and if by any chance this does not happen along the way, by the end of their days they will be overwhelmed by a deep sense of anguish and many existential questions will break into their minds. Eventually, they will realize their lives were devoid of meaning, there was no point, there was no purpose.

We know of hundreds of successful people, millionaires, even artists or business people who, due to this crisis, have taken their lives because they simply could not bear the pain of a meaningless life. They had great ability to manage their businesses and talents, to build fortunes, but they did not live the most important: the construction of meaningful and authentic relationships. Through their lives, they have changed the business, the music or the art world, but they could not change their own lives, because the meaning of our lives does not lie in things, my dear, but in the relationships we built during our lifetime.

The more meaning you bring to someone else's life, the more meaningful your own life gets. We were not created to be alone. In fact, we were not created to live this selfish life that we are encouraged to embrace every day, by this excessive consumerism advertised through endless mediums. Understand, the more you share of yourself, the more you have! The more you gain!

The more you devote yourself to fully live each moment of

your life with those you love, celebrating life at every meal, enjoying and taking care of them, being aware that you are writing the best moments of your story in these moments, the more your life will make sense, and you will be printing in the book of your life the memories you will also share with everyone you have been with.

Healers

Some people have the gift of making us feel more alive than ever. We leave their presence with an amazing will to live, we feel excited to work and to accomplish our dreams, we feel our batteries being recharged to face the hardest tasks. People like this are healers. Their presence heals us. Their words and affection are like medicine and they soothe our souls. Enlightened beings like these bring us good energy, we know that, as long as we are with them, we are going to LIVE, laugh, sing, talk, eat and become much better than when we were before. They bring meaning to our lives, even in the toughest days.

Conversely, there are people so toxic that the simple reminder of them or their words feel like a bell ringing out of tune, pestering our memories, bringing us anxiety and anguish, this is a display of how negative their presence is. They drain our energy, they take away from us the mood to laugh, to interact, to be ourselves. Others may even go as far as becoming torture machines, instilling psychological and/or physical violence, and being capable of taking away our will to live.

What about you?

What memories will you leave? When your friends and relatives hear the news of your death, do you think most people are going to cry? Will they miss you? Will they celebrate the privilege of having known you and having lived with you? Or will they sigh in relief, thinking that now they may have a chance to live, that they will no longer have to endure your presence or your words...

We are also the memories we leave behind, the emotions we brought to people.

You are what you sow!

You are what others feel in your presence!

Love or pain.

A source of hope or a source of despair.

Bitterness or kindness.

What memories will you print into other people's memories?

The point is, in the end, we must feel and know for sure that our lives were not in vain.

The biggest purpose of our lives

When we impact someone's life with love and dedication, we will automatically be a source of inspiration. Certainly, when we leave this place, this person who was influenced by us to become someone better will also become a source of happiness, life and inspiration for many other people, **and, just as tiny light sources we are, we will brighten and enlighten each other, and this world, which at times seems so dark and harsh, will become a beautiful bright place, filled with meaning**. I can say without a doubt, this is the biggest purpose of our lives.

We were created to love.

TO LOVE! To enlighten. To give ourselves. Because it is by giving that we will receive. When we help someone find meaning, meaning to their lives, by making them feel loved, accepted, and welcomed, our own lives will have a deeper meaning.

We were created to love. To give and to donate.

To love and to forgive.

We go through many afflictions in life, we are hurt, betrayed, other times we hurt others too. We need to learn the art of forgiving. Ourselves and others. A bitter and resented heart will not be able to love once more, to trust again. We need to learn to forgive, to leave the past behind, and to live lightly. Love is never heavy. If it feels that way, then it is not love. People tormented by resentment are heavy and harsh. To themselves and to others.

I believe this is the biggest purpose of our lives: learning how to love and to forgive. And loving so much to the point of becoming pure love. Giving yourself to life so much to the point of becoming life yourself. Laughing so much to the point of becoming laughter yourself. Living fully and intensely.

In the end, my dear, this is what makes our lives worth it.

Decide today to live your life to the fullest! Stop just existing!

Breathing just for breathing! Give meaning to your passage through this Earth so that YOU may make worthwhile this life that has been gifted to you.

Leave your mark in History, make the difference in someone else's life. **Live in such a way that when you die, you will be missed** in the heart of those who have been around you.

Be such an inspiration that others will also be willing to live their lives to the fullest, with the purpose of loving and helping even more people, and as we all go this path, we will form this collective awakening and everyone will become a beacon of light, bringing light to the chaos and darkness surrounding our Planet Earth.

Decide today that...

...I will let my little light shine.

Decide today...

...to be missed.

Personal analysis

Answer sincerely, you do not have to write it down, but you should reflect on it:

1. What memories/emotions will you be printing into the memories of those around you?

2. Do most people feel honored or suffocated by your presence?

3. When someone spends time with you, do they thank you when saying goodbye? Have you helped someone be a better person? Or feeling better in some way? Have you made someone's life lighter? Or maybe they have left your presence carrying an even bigger weight?

4. Our words create life or death. What are your words like?

5. Upon hearing news of your death, will most people cry? Will they miss you? Will they celebrate the privilege of having known you and having lived with you? Or will they sigh in relief, thinking that now they will have a chance to live?

Task

1. Write the story of your life while you can.

2. Make your existence valuable!

3. Remember, live in such a way that you will be missed!

Thoughts for meditation

*"Those who are wise will shine like
the brightness of the heavens, and those
who lead many to righteousness, like the
stars for ever and ever."*

Daniel 12:3

REFERENCES

The Message Study Bible Conversations Repack, Capturing the Notes and Reflections of Eugene Peterson. Navpress Pub Group, 2012.

COSTA. J. J. A sabedoria dos Ditados Populares [The Wisdom of Popular Sayings]. São Paulo: Butterfly, 2009.

Eco, Umberto, and Alastair McEwen. On the shoulders of giants. Cambridge, Massachusetts: The Belknap Press of Harvard University Press, 2019.

ONLINE REFERENCES

Research shows children whose parents nurture them early in life have enlarged brain regions linked to learning, memory, and response to stress. Available at <https://medicine.wustl.edu/news/love-and-the-hippocampus/> Accessed August 2020

BBC NEWS. The World Health Organization predicts that within 20 years more people will be affected by depression than any other health problem. Available at: <http://news.bbc.co.uk/2/hi/health/8230549.stm> Accessed August 2020.

Bible.com. Available at: <https://www.bible.com/bible/111/PSA.34.12-14.NIV>. Accessed September 2020.

Bible.com. Available at: <https://www.bible.com/bible/111/PRO.21.23.NIV>. Accessed September 2020.

QUODID. Available at: http://quodid.com/quotes/10572/dan-millman/every-positive-change-every-jump-to-a. Accessed August 2020.

HARVARD BUSINESS REVIEW. What VUCA Really Means for You. Available at <https://hbr.org/2014/01/what-vuca-really-me-ans-for-you. Accessed 15 December 2019.

COUNTRYLIVING.COM According to neuroscientists, this is the most important decision you'll ever make. Available at <https://www.countryliving.com/uk/wellbeing/news/a2213/most-important-

decision-who-you-spend-time-with/>. Accessed August 2020.

Sefaria.org. Psalms 1. Available at: <https://www.sefaria.org/Psalms.1?lang=bi> Accessed March 2021.

Vai trabalhar, Vagabundo! Chico Buarque's Song. Available at https://genius.com/Chico-buarque-vai-trabalhar-vagabundo-annotated. Accessed August 2020.

WeAreBrain.com. Adaptability: When change is the only constant. Available at:<https://www.wearebrain.com/blog/our-company/adaptability-when-change-is-the-only-constant/> Accessed August 2020.

THE AUTHOR

Jane Krüger is a living proof that it is possible to live to the fullest. Jane has three children, Esther, Samuel and Estevan. During her life, she went through countless adversities, overcoming one after another, with untamed determination and tenacity, having helped, along her journey, thousands of people to find meaning among pain, making them stand up even stronger and more resilient, no matter what they have been through. In this book, she sums up her experiences in 21 chapters that will completely transform your own story.

Jane Krüger is a psychoanalyst, psychopedagogist, researcher, teacher and composer.

 /dra.janekruger

 /dra.janekruger | dr.janekruger

 /drajanekruger